www.EffortlessMath.com

… So Much More Online!

✓ FREE Math lessons

✓ More Math learning books!

✓ Mathematics Worksheets

✓ Online Math Tutors

Need a PDF version of this book?

Visit www.EffortlessMath.com

Or send email to: info@EffortlessMath.com

Algebra I Exercise Book: Student Workbook

By

Reza Nazari

& Ava Ross

Copyright © 2019

Reza Nazari & Ava Ross

All inquiries should be addressed to:

info@effortlessMath.com

www.EffortlessMath.com

ISBN-13: 978-1-970036-91-6

ISBN-10: 1-970036-91-5

Published by: Effortless Math Education

www.EffortlessMath.com

Description

This Algebra I workbook's new edition has been updated to replicate questions appearing on the most recent Algebra I test. Here is intensive preparation for the Algebra I course, and a precious learning tool for Algebra takers who need extra practice in math to raise their Algebra I scores. After completing this workbook, you will have solid foundation and adequate practice that is necessary to ace the Algebra I Test. **This workbook is your ticket to score higher on Algebra I test.**

The updated version of this hands-on workbook represents extensive exercises, math problems, sample Algebra I questions, and quizzes with answers and detailed solutions to help you hone your math skills, overcome your exam anxiety, and boost your confidence -- and do your best to defeat Algebra I exam on test day.

Each of math exercises is answered in the book which will help you find your weak areas and raise your scores. This is a unique and perfect practice book to beat the Algebra I Test.

Separate math chapters offer a complete review of the Algebra course, including:

- Functions and their applications
- Expressions and Equations
- Inequalities and System of Equations
- Quadratic and Polynomial Operations
- Radical Expressions
- … and many more Algebra I topics

The surest way to succeed on Algebra I is with intensive practice in every math topic tested--and that's what you will get in *Algebra I Exercise Book*. Each chapter of this focused format has a comprehensive review created by Math experts that goes into detail to cover all of the content likely to appear on the Algebra I test.

Effortless Math Workbook for the Algebra I contains many exciting and unique features to help you improve your Algebra scores, including:

- Content 100% aligned with the Algebra I courses
- Written by experienced Math tutors and test experts
- Complete coverage of all Algebra I concepts and topics which you will be tested
- Over 2,500 additional Algebra I math practice questions in both multiple-choice and grid-in formats with answers grouped by topic, so you can focus on your weak areas
- Abundant Math skill building exercises to help you approach different question types that might be unfamiliar to you
- Exercises on different Algebra I topics such as equations, polynomials, exponents and radicals, functions, etc.

This Algebra I Workbook and other Effortless Math Education books are used by thousands of students each year to help them review core content areas, brush-up in math, discover their strengths and weaknesses, and achieve their best scores on the Algebra test.

Get ready for the Algebra Test with a PERFECT Workbook!

About the Author

Reza Nazari is the author of more than 100 Math learning books including:
– **Math and Critical Thinking Challenges:** For the Middle and High School Student
– **GED Math in 30 Days**
– **ASVAB Math Workbook 2018 - 2019**
– **Effortless Math Education Workbooks**
– **and many more Mathematics books ...**

Reza is also an experienced Math instructor and a test–prep expert who has been tutoring students since 2008. Reza is the founder of Effortless Math Education, a tutoring company that has helped many students raise their standardized test scores—and attend the colleges of their dreams. Reza provides an individualized custom learning plan and the personalized attention that makes a difference in how students view math.

You can contact Reza via email at:
reza@EffortlessMath.com

Find Reza's professional profile at:
goo.gl/zoC9rJ

Contents

Chapter 1: The Basics

Topics that you'll learn in this chapter:

- ✓ Translate Phrases into an Algebraic Statement
- ✓ Order of Operations
- ✓ Properties of Numbers
- ✓ The Distributive Property

Translate Phrases into an Algebraic Statement

✎ *Write an algebraic expression for each phrase.*

1) 4 multiplied by x. _____

2) Subtract 8 from y. _____

3) 6 divided by x. _____

4) 12 decreased by y. _____

5) Add y to 9. _____

6) The square of 5. _____

7) x raised to the fourth power. _____

8) The sum of nine and a number. _____

9) The difference between sixty–four and y. _____

10) The quotient of twelve and a number. _____

11) The quotient of the square of x and 7. _____

12) The difference between x and 8 is 22. _____

13) 2 times a reduced by the square of b. _____

14) Subtract the product of a and b from 12. _____

Order of Operations

✎ *Evaluate each expression.*

1) $5 + (4 \times 2) =$

2) $13 - (2 \times 5) =$

3) $(16 \times 2) + 18 =$

4) $(12 - 5) - (4 \times 3) =$

5) $25 + (14 \div 2) =$

6) $(18 \times 5) \div 5 =$

7) $(48 \div 2) \times (-4) =$

8) $(7 \times 5) + (25 - 12) =$

9) $64 + (3 \times 2) + 8 =$

10) $(20 \times 5) \div (4 + 1) =$

11) $(-9) + (12 \times 6) + 15 =$

12) $(7 \times 8) - (56 \div 4) =$

13) $(4 \times 8 \div 2) - (17 + 11) =$

14) $(18 + 8 - 15) \times 5 - 3 =$

15) $(25 - 12 + 45) \times (95 \div 5) =$

16) $28 + \big(15 - (32 \div 2)\big) =$

17) $(6 + 7 - 4 - 9) + (18 \div 2) =$

18) $(95 - 17) + (10 - 25 + 9) =$

19) $(18 \times 2) + (15 \times 5) - 12 =$

20) $12 + 8 - (42 \times 4) + 50 =$

Properties of Numbers

✎ **Evaluate each expression. Name the property used in each step.**

1) $3 [4 - 2 \times 6] \div 6$

2) $5 (6 + 8) \times 12$

3) $3 + 6 \times 12$

4) $15 - (6 - 2) \times 10$

5) $6 [2 - (10 \div 2)]$

6) $4 (9 \div 3 - 7) \times \frac{1}{2}$

7) $8 + 12 [5 - 3(4 + 6)]$

8) $6 + 2 (18 - 3^2) - 4$

9) $4 (12 - 42 \div 3) + 3 \times \frac{4}{3}$

10) $5 (27 \div 3^2)$

✎ **Find the value of x.**

11) $5 (2 \times 6) = 2 (x \times 5)$

12) $(1 \times 5) 7 = (7 \times 1) x$

13) $(9 \times 1) 6 = x (9 \times 6)$

14) $(x \times 0) 10 = (4 \times 10) 0$

15) $(3 \times 1) 5 = (x \times 3)$

16) $(9 \times 3) 10 = x (10 \times 9)$

The Distributive Property

✎ *Use the distributive property to simply each expression.*

1) $2(2 + 3x) =$

2) $3(5 + 5x) =$

3) $4(3x - 8) =$

4) $(6x - 2)(-2) =$

5) $(-3)(x + 2) =$

6) $(2 + 2x)5 =$

7) $(-4)(4 - 2x) =$

8) $-(-2 - 5x) =$

9) $(-6x + 2)(-1) =$

10) $(-5)(x - 2) =$

11) $-(7 - 3x) =$

12) $8(8 + 2x) =$

13) $2(12 + 2x) =$

14) $(-6x + 8)4 =$

15) $(3 - 6x)(-7) =$

16) $(-12)(2x + 1) =$

17) $(8 - 2x)9 =$

18) $5(7 + 9x) =$

19) $11(5x + 2) =$

20) $(-4x + 6)6 =$

21) $(3 - 6x)(-8) =$

22) $(-12)(2x - 3) =$

23) $(10 - 2x)9 =$

24) $(-5)(11x - 2) =$

25) $(1 - 9x)(-10) =$

26) $(-6)(x + 8) =$

27) $(-4 + 3x)(-8) =$

28) $(-5)(1 - 11x) =$

29) $11(3x - 12) =$

30) $(-12x + 14)(-5) =$

31) $(-5)(4x - 1) + 4(x + 2) =$

32) $(-3)(x + 4) - (2 + 3x) =$

Scientific Notation

✎ **Write each number in scientific notation.**

1) $0.113 =$

2) $0.02 =$

3) $2.5 =$

4) $20 =$

5) $60 =$

6) $0.004 =$

7) $78 =$

8) $1,600 =$

9) $1,450 =$

10) $91,000 =$

11) $2,000,000 =$

12) $0.0000006 =$

13) $354,000 =$

14) $0.000325 =$

15) $0.00023 =$

16) $56,000,000 =$

17) $21,000 =$

18) $78,000,000 =$

19) $0.0000022 =$

20) $0.00012 =$

✎ **Write each number in standard notation.**

21) $3 \times 10^{-1} =$

22) $5 \times 10^{-2} =$

23) $1.2 \times 10^3 =$

24) $2 \times 10^{-4} =$

25) $1.5 \times 10^{-2} =$

26) $4 \times 10^3 =$

27) $9 \times 10^5 =$

28) $1.12 \times 10^4 =$

29) $3 \times 10^{-5} =$

30) $8.3 \times 10^{-5} =$

Answers of Worksheets – Chapter 1

Translate Phrases into an Algebraic Statement

1) $4x$
2) $y - 8$
3) $\frac{6}{x}$
4) $12 - y$
5) $y + 9$

6) 5^2
7) x^4
8) $9 + x$
9) $64 - y$
10) $\frac{12}{x}$

11) $\frac{x^2}{7}$
12) $x - 8 = 22$
13) $2a - b^2$
14) $12 - ab$

Order of Operations

1) 13
2) 3
3) 50
4) -5
5) 32
6) 18
7) -96

8) 48
9) 78
10) 20
11) 78
12) 42
13) -12
14) 52

15) 1,102
16) 27
17) 9
18) 72
19) 99
20) -98

Properties of Numbers

1) -4

2) 840

3) 75

4) 25

5) -18

6) -8

7) -292

8) 20

9) -4

10) 15

11) 6

12) 5

13) 1

14) 0

15) 5

16) 3

The Distributive Property

1) $6x + 4$
2) $15x + 15$
3) $12x - 32$
4) $-12x + 4$
5) $-3x - 6$
6) $10x + 10$
7) $8x - 16$

8) $5x + 2$
9) $6x - 2$
10) $-5x + 10$
11) $3x - 7$
12) $16x + 64$
13) $4x + 24$
14) $-24x + 32$

15) $42x - 21$
16) $-24x - 12$
17) $-18x + 72$
18) $45x + 35$
19) $55x + 22$
20) $-24x + 36$
21) $48x - 24$

22) $-24x + 36$

23) $-18x + 90$

24) $-55x + 10$

25) $90x - 10$

26) $-6x - 48$

27) $-24x + 32$

28) $55x - 5$

29) $33x - 132$

30) $60x - 70$

31) $-16x + 13$

32) $-6x - 14$

Equations

1) $\{20\}$

2) $\{-16\}$

3) $\{1\}$

4) $\{-4\}$

5) $\{-4\}$

6) $\{4\}$

7) $\{12\}$

8) $\{-9\}$

9) $\{1\}$

10) $\{0\}$

11) $7 = x$

12) $-4 = x$

13) $30 = y$

14) $\frac{5}{56} = x$

15) $5 = y$

16) $\frac{1}{2} = x$

17) $27 = y$

18) $3 = y$

19) $x = -3$

20) $x = 55$

Scientific Notation

1) 1.13×10^{-1}

2) 2×10^{-2}

3) 2.5×10^{0}

4) 2×10^{1}

5) 6×10^{1}

6) 4×10^{-3}

7) 7.8×10^{1}

8) 1.6×10^{3}

9) 1.45×10^{3}

10) 9.1×10^{4}

11) 2×10^{6}

12) 6×10^{-7}

13) 3.54×10^{5}

14) 3.25×10^{-4}

15) 2.3×10^{-4}

16) 5.6×10^{7}

17) 2.1×10^{4}

18) 7.8×10^{7}

19) 2.2×10^{-6}

20) 1.2×10^{-4}

21) 0.3

22) 0.05

23) $1,200$

24) 0.0002

25) 0.015

26) $4,000$

27) $900,000$

28) $11,200$

29) 0.00003

30) 0.000083

Chapter 2: Expressions and Equations

Topics that you'll learn in this chapter:

- ✓ Simplify Expressions
- ✓ One–step Equations
- ✓ Multi–step Equations
- ✓ Finding Midpoint
- ✓ Finding Distance between Two Points
- ✓ Absolute Value Equations

Simplifying Variable Expressions

✍ *Simplify each expression.*

1) $3(x + 9) =$

2) $(-6)(8x - 4) =$

3) $7x + 3 - 3x =$

4) $-2 - x^2 - 6x^2 =$

5) $3 + 10x^2 + 2 =$

6) $8x^2 + 6x + 7x^2 =$

7) $5x^2 - 12x^2 + 8x =$

8) $2x^2 - 2x - x =$

9) $4x + 6(2 - 5x) =$

10) $10x + 8(10x - 6) =$

11) $9(-2x - 6) - 5 =$

12) $2x^2 + (-8x) =$

13) $x - 3 + 5 - 3x =$

14) $2 - 3x + 12 - 2x =$

15) $32x - 4 + 23 + 2x =$

16) $(-6)(8x - 4) + 10x =$

17) $14x - 5(5 - 8x) =$

18) $23x + 4(9x + 3) + 12 =$

19) $3(-7x + 5) + 20x =$

20) $12x - 3x(x + 9) =$

21) $7x + 5x(3 - 3x) =$

22) $5x(-8x + 12) + 14x =$

23) $40x + 12 + 2x^2 =$

24) $5x(x - 3) - 10 =$

25) $8x - 7 + 8x + 2x^2 =$

26) $2x^2 - 5x - 7x =$

27) $7x - 3x^2 - 5x^2 - 3 =$

28) $4 + x^2 - 6x^2 - 12x =$

29) $12x + 8x^2 + 2x + 20 =$

30) $2x^2 + 6x + 3x^2 =$

31) $23 + 15x^2 + 8x - 4x^2 =$

32) $8x - 12x - x^2 + 13 =$

One–Step Equations

✎ *Solve each equation.*

1) $2x = 20, x = $ ____

2) $4x = 16, x = $ ____

3) $8x = 24, x = $ ____

4) $6x = 30, x = $ ____

5) $x + 5 = 8, x = $ ____

6) $x - 1 = 5, x = $ ____

7) $x - 8 = 3, x = $ ____

8) $x + 6 = 12, x = $ ____

9) $x - 2 = 17, x = $ ____

10) $8 = 12 + x, x = $ ____

11) $x - 5 = 4, x = $ ____

12) $2 - x = -12, x = $ ____

13) $16 = -4 + x, x = $ ____

14) $x - 4 = -25, x = $ ____

15) $x + 12 = -9, x = $ ____

16) $14 = 18 - x, x = $ ____

17) $2 + x = -14, x = $ ____

18) $x - 5 = 15, x = $ ____

19) $25 = x - 5, x = $ ____

20) $x - 3 = -12, x = $ ____

21) $x - 12 = 12, x = $ ____

22) $x - 12 = -25, x = $ ____

23) $x - 13 = 32, x = $ ____

24) $-55 = x - 18, x = $ ____

25) $x - 12 = 18, x = $ ____

26) $20 = 5x, x = $ ____

27) $x - 30 = 20, x = $ ____

28) $x - 12 = 32, x = $ ____

29) $36 - x = 3, x = $ ____

30) $x - 14 = 14, x = $ ____

31) $19 - x = -15, x = $ ____

32) $x - 19 = -35, x = $ ____

Multi–Step Equations

✎ **Solve each equation.**

1) $2x + 3 = 5$

2) $-x + 8 = 5$

3) $3x - 4 = 5$

4) $-(2 - x) = 5$

5) $2x - 18 = 12$

6) $4x - 2 = 6$

7) $2x - 14 = 4$

8) $5x + 10 = 25$

9) $8x + 9 = 25$

10) $-3(2 + x) = 3$

11) $-2(4 + x) = 4$

12) $20 = -(x - 8)$

13) $2(2 - 2x) = 20$

14) $-12 = -(2x + 8)$

15) $5(2 + x) = 5$

16) $2(x - 14) = 4$

17) $-28 = 2x + 12x$

18) $3x + 15 = -x - 5$

19) $2(3 + 2x) = -18$

20) $12 - 2x = -8 - x$

21) $10 - 3x = 14 + x$

22) $10 + 10x = -2 + 4x$

23) $24 = (-4x) - 8 + 8$

24) $12 = 2x - 12 + 6x$

25) $-12 = -4x - 6 + 2x$

26) $4x - 12 = -18 + 5x$

27) $5x - 10 = 2x + 5$

28) $-7 - 3x = 2(3 - 2x)$

29) $x - 2 = -3(6 - 3x)$

30) $10x - 56 = 12x - 114$

31) $4x - 8 = -4(11 + 2x)$

32) $-5x - 14 = 6x + 52$

Finding Midpoint

✎ *Find the midpoint of the line segment with the given endpoints.*

1) $(-2, -2), (0, 2)$

2) $(5, 1), (-2, 4)$

3) $(4, -1), (0, 3)$

4) $(-3, 5), (-1, 3)$

5) $(3, -2), (7, -6)$

6) $(-4, -3), (2, -7)$

7) $(5, 0), (-5, 8)$

8) $(-6, 4), (-2, 0)$

9) $(-3, 4), (9, -6)$

10) $(2, 8), (6, -2)$

11) $(4, 7), (-6, 5)$

12) $(9, 3), (-1, -7)$

13) $(-4, 12), (-2, 6)$

14) $(14, 5), (8, -1)$

15) $(11, 7), (-3, 1)$

16) $(-7, -4), (-3, 8)$

17) $(13, 7), (5, 11)$

18) $(-5, -10), (9, -2)$

19) $(8, 15), (-2, 7)$

20) $(13, -2), (5, 10)$

21) $(2, -2), (3, -5)$

22) $(0, 2), (-2, -6)$

23) $(7, 4), (9, -1)$

24) $(4, -5), (0, 8)$

✎ *Solve each problem.*

25) One endpoint of a line segment is $(1, 2)$ and the midpoint of the line segment is $(-1, 4)$. What is the other endpoint? _____

26) One endpoint of a line segment is $(-3, 6)$ and the midpoint of the line segment is $(5, 2)$. What is the other endpoint? _____

27) One endpoint of a line segment is $(-2, -6)$ and the midpoint of the line segment is $(6, 8)$. What is the other endpoint? _____

Finding Distance of Two Points

✎ **Find the distance between each pair of points.**

1) $(2, 1), (-1, -3)$

2) $(-2, -1), (2, 2)$

3) $(-1, 0), (5, 8)$

4) $(-4, -1), (1, 11)$

5) $(3, -2), (-6, -14)$

6) $(-6, 0), (-2, 3)$

7) $(3, 2), (11, 17)$

8) $(-6, -10), (6, -1)$

9) $(5, 9), (-11, -3)$

10) $(9, -3), (3, -11)$

11) $(2, 0), (12, 24)$

12) $(8, 4), (3, -8)$

13) $(4, 2), (-5, -10)$

14) $(-5, 6), (3, 21)$

15) $(0, 8), (-4, 5)$

16) $(-8, -5), (4, 0)$

17) $(3, 5), (-5, -10)$

18) $(-2, 3), (22, 13)$

19) $(7, 2), (-8, -18)$

20) $(-5, 4), (7, 9)$

✎ **Solve each problem.**

21) Triangle ABC is a right triangle on the coordinate system and its vertices are $(-2, 5)$, $(-2, 1)$, and $(1, 1)$. What is the area of triangle ABC? _____

22) Three vertices of a triangle on a coordinate system are $(1, 1)$, $(1, 4)$, and $(5, 4)$. What is the perimeter of the triangle? _____

23) Four vertices of a rectangle on a coordinate system are $(2, 5)$, $(2, 2)$, $(6, 5)$, and $(6, 2)$. What is its perimeter? _____

Absolute Value Equations

✏️ *Evaluate the value.*

1) $|n| + 1 = 2$

2) $|m| + 2 = 11$

3) $-3|p| = -12$

4) $|7m| + 3 = 73$

5) $-10|v + 2| = -70$

6) $4|n + 8| = 56$

7) $|6m| = 42$

8) $|k + 8| - 5 = 2$

9) $3|-8x| + 8 = 80$

10) $2 - 5|5x - 5| = -73$

11) $5|-2x - 1| = 10$

12) $|x - 10| = 3$

13) $|-7x| - 24 = 23$

14) $6|x - 25| = 26$

15) $|-2| - \frac{|-10|}{2} =$

16) $8 - |2 - 14| - |-2| =$

17) $\frac{|-36|}{6} \times |-6| =$

18) $\frac{|5 \times -3|}{5} \times \frac{|-20|}{4} =$

19) $|2 \times -4| + \frac{|-40|}{5} =$

20) $\frac{|-28|}{4} \times \frac{|-55|}{11} =$

21) $|-12 + 4| \times \frac{|-4 \times 5|}{2}$

22) $\frac{|-10 \times 3|}{2} \times |-12| =$

✏️ *Evaluate each expression if* $a = -2$, $b = 3$ *and* $c = -4.2$

23) $2a + (b + 3) =$

24) $5 - |c + 1| =$

25) $|a + b| - c =$

26) $|b + 1| + 8 =$

Answers of Worksheets – Chapter 2

Simplifying Variable Expressions

1) $3x + 27$
2) $-48x + 24$
3) $4x + 3$
4) $-7x^2 - 2$
5) $10x^2 + 5$
6) $15x^2 + 6x$
7) $-7x^2 + 8x$
8) $2x^2 - 3x$
9) $-24x + 12$
10) $90x - 48$
11) $-18x - 59$
12) $2x^2 - 8x$
13) $-2x + 2$
14) $-5x + 14$
15) $34x + 19$
16) $-38x + 24$
17) $54x - 25$
18) $59x + 24$
19) $-x + 15$
20) $-3x^2 - 15x$
21) $-15x^2 + 22x$
22) $-40x^2 + 74x$
23) $2x^2 + 40x + 12$
24) $5x^2 - 15x - 10$
25) $2x^2 + 16x - 7$
26) $2x^2 - 12x$
27) $-8x^2 + 7x - 3$
28) $-5x^2 - 12x + 4$
29) $8x^2 + 14x + 20$
30) $5x^2 + 6x$
31) $11x^2 + 8x + 23$
32) $-x^2 - 4x + 13$

One–Step Equations

1) 10
2) 4
3) 3
4) 5
5) 3
6) 6
7) 11
8) 6
9) 19
10) -4
11) 9
12) 14
13) 20
14) -21
15) -21
16) 4
17) -16
18) 20
19) 30
20) -9
21) 24
22) -13
23) 45
24) -37
25) 30
26) 4
27) 50
28) 42
29) 33
30) 28
31) 34
32) -16

Multi–Step Equations

1) 1
2) 3
3) 3
4) 7
5) 15
6) 2
7) 9
8) 3
9) 2
10) -3
11) -6
12) -12
13) -4
14) 2
15) -1
16) 16
17) -2
18) -5
19) -6
20) 20
21) -1
22) -2
23) -6
24) 3
25) 3
26) 6
27) 5
28) 13
29) 2
30) 29

31) -3

32) -6

Finding Midpoint

1) $(-1, 0)$

2) $(1.5, 2.5)$

3) $(2, 1)$

4) $(-2, 4)$

5) $(5, -4)$

6) $(-1, -5)$

7) $(0, 4)$

8) $(-4, 2)$

9) $(3, -1)$

10) $(4, 3)$

11) $(-1, 6)$

12) $(4, -2)$

13) $(-3, 9)$

14) $(11, 2)$

15) $(4, 4)$

16) $(-5, 2)$

17) $(9, 9)$

18) $(2, -6)$

19) $(3, 11)$

20) $(9, 4)$

21) $(2.5, -3.5)$

22) $(-1, -2)$

23) $(8, 1.5)$

24) $(2, 1.5)$

25) $(-3, 6)$

26) $(13, -2)$

27) $(14, 22)$

Finding Distance of Two Points

1) 5

2) 5

3) 10

4) 13

5) 15

6) 5

7) 17

8) 15

9) 20

10) 10

11) 26

12) 13

13) 15

14) 17

15) 5

16) 13

17) 17

18) 26

19) 25

20) 13

21) 6 *square units*

22) 12 *units*

23) 14 *units*

Absolute value equations

1) $\{1, -1\}$

2) $\{9, -9\}$

3) $\{4, -4\}$

4) $\{10, -10\}$

5) $\{5, -9\}$

6) $\{6, -22\}$

7) $\{7, -7\}$

8) $\{-1, -15\}$

9) $\{-3, 3\}$

10) $\{4, -2\}$

11) $\{-6, 5\}$

12) $\{13, 7\}$

13) $\{6.71, -6.71\}$

14) $\{29.33, 20.67\}$

15) -3

16) -6

17) 36

18) 15

19) 16

20) 35

21) 80

22) 180

23) 8

24) 1.8

25) 5.2

26) 12

Chapter 3:
Linear Functions

Topics that you'll practice in this chapter:

- ✓ Finding Slope
- ✓ Graphing Lines Using Line Equation
- ✓ Writing Linear Equations
- ✓ Graphing Linear Inequalities
- ✓ Slope and Rate of Change
- ✓ Find the Slope, x–intercept and y–intercept
- ✓ Write an Equation from a Graph
- ✓ Slope–intercept Form and Point–slope Form
- ✓ Equations of Horizontal and Vertical Lines
- ✓ Equation of Parallel or Perpendicular Lines
- ✓ Graphing Absolute Value Equations

Finding Slope

✍ *Find the slope of each line.*

1) $y = x - 1$

2) $y = -2x + 5$

3) $y = 2x - 1$

4) $y = -x - 8$

5) $y = 6 + 5x$

6) $y = 2 - 3x$

7) $y = 4x + 12$

8) $y = -6x + 2$

9) $y = -x + 8$

10) $y = 7x - 5$

11) $y = \frac{1}{2}x + 3$

12) $y = -\frac{2}{3}x + 1$

13) $-x + 2y = 5$

14) $2x + 2y = 6$

15) $8y - 2x = 10$

16) $5y - x = 2$

✍ *Find the slope of the line through each pair of points.*

17) $(1, 1), (2, 3)$

18) $(-1, 2), (0, 3)$

19) $(3, -1), (2, 3)$

20) $(-2, -1), (0, 5)$

21) $(5, 1), (2, 4)$

22) $(-3, 1), (-2, 4)$

23) $(6, 2), (7, 4)$

24) $(6, -5), (3, 4)$

25) $(12, -9), (11, -8)$

26) $(7, 4), (5, -2)$

27) $(1, 1), (3, 5)$

28) $(7, -12), (5, 10)$

Graphing Lines Using Line Equation

✍ *Sketch the graph of each line.*

1) $y = 3x - 2$

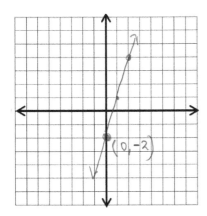

2) $y = -x + 1$

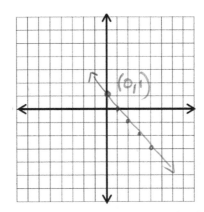

3) $x + y = 4$ $y = -x + 4$

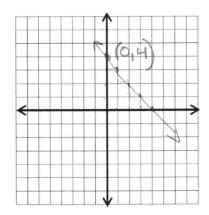

4) $x - y = -5$

$$x - y = -5$$
$$-y = -x - 5$$
$$y = x + 5$$

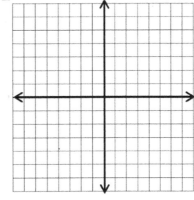

5) $y = -x + 4$

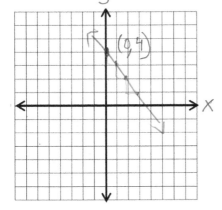

6) $y = 2x + 5$

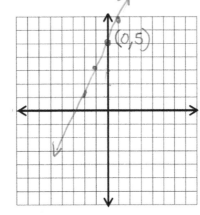

Writing Linear Equations

✍ *Write the slope–intercept form of the equation of the line through the given points*

1) through: $(1, -2), (2, 3)$

2) through: $(-2, 1), (1, 4)$

3) through: $(-2, 1), (0, 5)$

4) through: $(5, 4), (2, 1)$

5) through: $(-4, 9), (3, 2)$

6) through: $(8, 3), (7, 2)$

7) through: $(7, -2), (5, 2)$

8) through: $(-3, 9), (5, -7)$

9) through: $(6, 8), (4, 14)$

10) through: $(5, 9), (7, -3)$

11) through: $(-2, 8), (-6, -4)$

12) through: $(3, 3), (1, -5)$

13) through: $(8, -5), (-5, 8)$

14) through: $(2, -6), (-1, 3)$

15) through: $(5, 5), (2, -4)$

16) through: $(-1, 8), (2, -7)$

17) through: $(12, 4), (10, -4)$

18) through: $(8, -1), (7, -6)$

19) through: $(1, -2), (2, 3)$

20) through: $(-1, 1), (-2, 6)$

21) through: $(0, 3), (-4, -1)$

22) through: $(0, 2), (1, -3)$

23) through: $(0, -5), (4, 3)$

24) through: $(-1, 4), (0, 4)$

25) through: $(2, -3), (3, -5)$

26) through: $(2, 5), (-1, -4)$

27) through: $(1, -3), (-3, 1)$

28) through: $(4, 4), (3, -5)$

29) through: $(0, 3), (1, 1)$

30) through: $(5, 5), (2, -3)$

31) through: $(-2, -2), (2, -5)$

32) through: $(-3, -2), (1, -1)$

Graphing Linear Inequalities

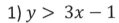

✏ *Sketch the graph of each linear inequality.*

1) $y > 3x - 1$

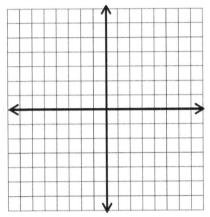

2) $y < -x + 4$

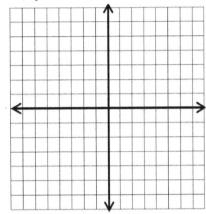

3) $y \leq -5x + 8$

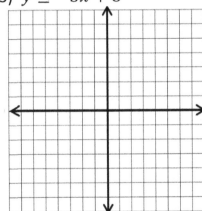

4) $2y \geq 8 + 6x$

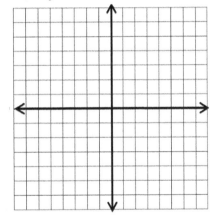

5) $y \geq -3 + 5x$

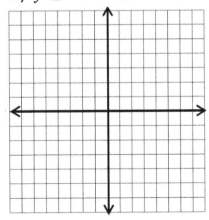

6) $y \geq 5 - 7x$

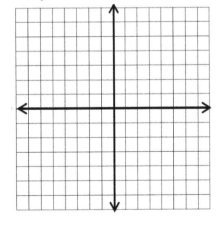

Slope and Rate of Change

Example:

Rate of change in the first graph is 1 and in the second graph is 1/3.

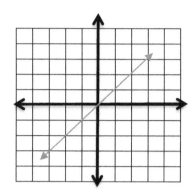 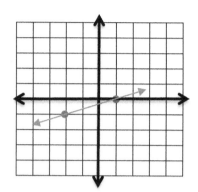

✎ **Find the slope of the line that passes through the points.**

1) $(5, -2), (5, 8)$

2) $(1, 2), (7, 7)$

3) $(3, 0), (-5, -4)$

4) $(5, 9), (3, 9)$

5) $(12, 10), (12, 5)$

6) $(0.2, -0.9), (0.5, -0.9)$

7) $(7, -4), (4, 8)$

8) $(15, 2), (-6, 5)$

✎ **Find the value of r so the line that passes through each pair of points has the given slope.**

9) $(r, 7), (11, 8), m = \frac{1}{3}$

$$\frac{8-7}{11-r} = \frac{1}{3}$$

10) $(-5, r), (1, 3), m = \frac{7}{6}$

11) $(-7, 2), (-8, r), m = 5$

12) $(r, 2), (5, r), m = 0$

Find the Slope, x–intercept and y–intercept

✎ *Find the* x *and* y *intercepts for the following equations.*

1) $x + 7y = 10$

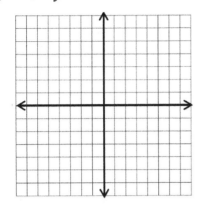

2) $y = x + 3$

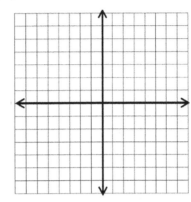

3) $4x = 2y + 6$

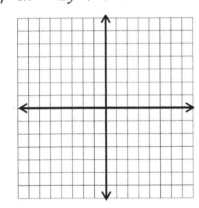

4) $5 - 2y = 3x$

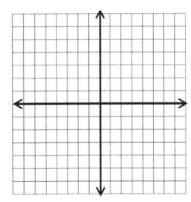

5) $5x - 2y = 7$

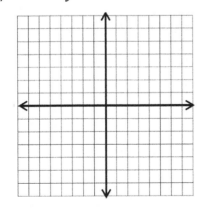

6) $y = 4 + x$

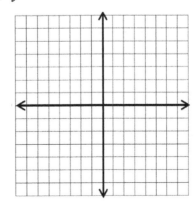

Write an Equation from a Graph

✍ *Write the slope intercept form of the equation of each line.*

1) _____

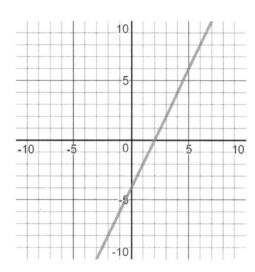

2) _____

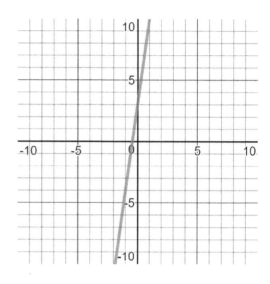

3) _____

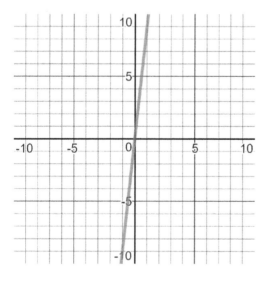

4) _____

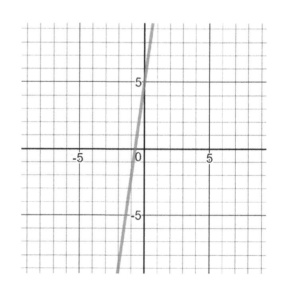

Slope–intercept Form and Point–slope Form

✎ *Write the slope–intercept form of the equation of each line.*

1) $-14x + y = 7$

2) $-2(2x + y) = 28$

3) $-11x - 7y = -56$

4) $9x + 35 = -5y$

5) $x - 3y = 6$

6) $13x - 11y = -12$

7) $11x - 8y = -48$

8) $3x - 2y = -16$

9) $2y = -6x - 8$

10) $2y = -4x + 10$

11) $2y = -2x - 4$

12) $6x + 5y = -15$

✎ *Find the slope of the following lines. Name a point on each line.*

7) $y = 2(x + 3)$

8) $y + 2 = \frac{2}{3}(x - 4)$

9) $y + 3 = -1.5x$

10) $y - 3 = \frac{1}{2}(x - 3)$

11) $y + 2 = 1.3(x + 1)$

12) $y - 5 = 3x$

13) $y - 3 = -2(x - 4)$

14) $y + 3 = 0$

15) $y + 2 = 3(x + 6)$

16) $y - 7 = -4(x - 2)$

✎ *Write an equation in point–slope form for the line that passes through the given point with the slope provided.*

17) $(1, 2), m = 7$

18) $(3, 5), m = \frac{5}{3}$

19) $(2, -4), m = -1$

20) $(-1, 2), m = 2$

21) $(-1, 4), m = 4$

22) $(-1, 2), m = 2$

23) $(3, 1), m = \frac{1}{2}$

24) $(-2, 5), m = -4$

Equations of Horizontal and Vertical Lines

✎ *Sketch the graph of each line.*

1) $y = 0$

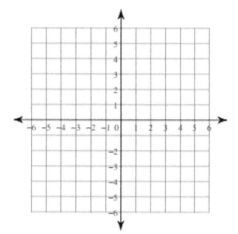

2) $y = 2$

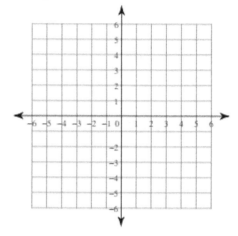

3) $x = -4$

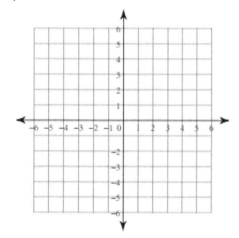

4) $x = 3$

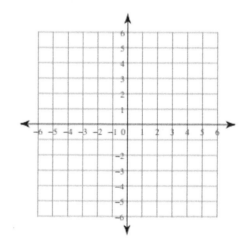

5) $y = -5$

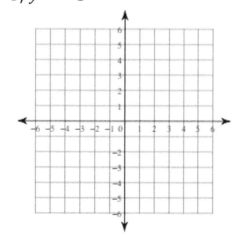

6) $x = 2$

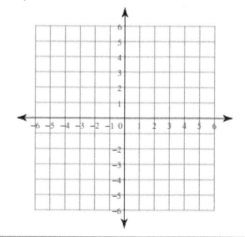

Equation of Parallel or Perpendicular Lines

✍ *Write an equation of the line that passes through the given point and is parallel to the given line.*

1) $(-2, -4), 4x + 7y = -14$

2) $(-4, 2), y = -x + 3$

3) $(-2, 5), 2y = 4x - 6$

4) $(-10, 0), -y + 3x = 16$

5) $(5, -1), y = -\frac{3}{5}x - 3$

6) $(1, 7), -6x + y = -1$

7) $(2, -3), y = \frac{1}{5}x + 5$

8) $(1, 4), -6x + 5y = -10$

9) $(3, -3), y = -\frac{5}{2}x - 1$

10) $(-4, 3), 2x + 3y = -9$

✍ *Write an equation of the line that passes through the given point and is perpendicular to the given line.*

11) $(-1, -7), 3x + 12y = -6$

12) $(-3, 5), 5x - 6y = 9$

13) $(2, 6), y = -3$

14) $(-2, 3), x = 4$

15) $(1, -5), y = \frac{1}{8}x + 2$

16) $(3, 4), y = -2x - 4$

17) $(-5, 5), y = \frac{5}{9}x - 4$

18) $(4, -1), y = x + 2$

Graphing Absolute Value Equations

✎ *Graph each equation.*

1) $y = |x + 4|$

2) $y = |x + 1|$

3) $y = -|x| - 1$

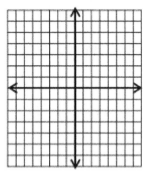

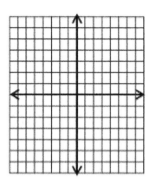

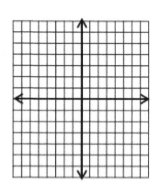

4) $y = |x - 2|$

5) $y = -|x - 2|$

6) $y = -2|2x + 2| + 4$

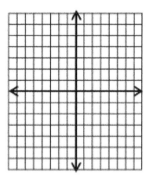

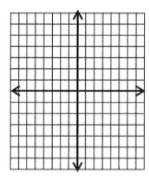

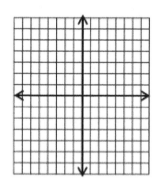

Answers of Worksheets – Chapter 3

Finding Slope

1) 1
2) −2
3) 2
4) −1
5) 5
6) −4
7) 3
8) −6
9) −1
10) 7

11) $\frac{1}{2}$
12) $-\frac{2}{3}$
13) $-\frac{1}{2}$
14) −1
15) $\frac{1}{4}$
16) $\frac{1}{5}$
17) 2
18) 1

19) −4
20) 3
21) −1
22) 3
23) 2
24) −3
25) −1
26) 3
27) 2
28) −11

Graphing Lines Using Line Equation

1)

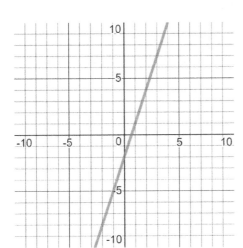

2)

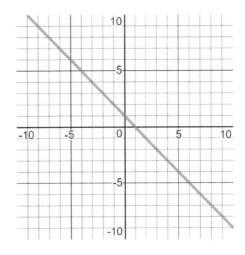

3)

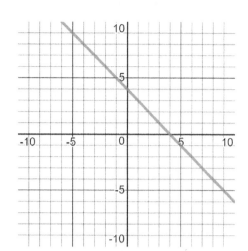

4)

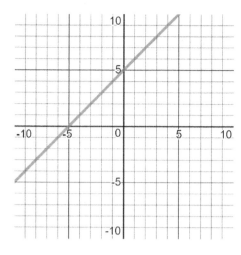

5)

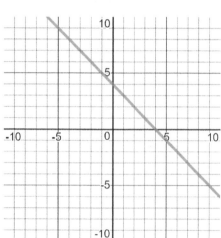

6)

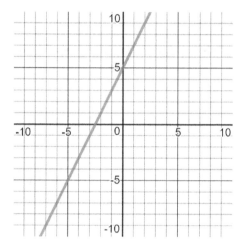

Writing Linear Equations

1) $y = 5x - 7$

2) $y = x + 3$

3) $y = 2x + 5$

4) $y = x - 1$

5) $y = -x + 5$

6) $y = x - 5$

7) $y = -2x + 12$

8) $y = -2x + 3$

9) $y = -3x + 26$

10) $y = -6x + 39$

11) $y = 3x + 14$

12) $y = 4x - 9$

13) $y = -x + 3$

14) $y = -3x$

15) $y = 3x - 10$

16) $y = -5x + 3$

17) $y = 4x - 44$

18) $y = 5x - 41$

19) $y = 7x + 26$ -7

20) $y = -5x - 4$

21) $y = x + 3$

22) $y = -5x + 2$

23) $y = 2x - 5$

24) $y = 4$

25) $y = -2x + 1$

26) $y = 3x - 1$

27) $y = -x - 2$

28) $y = 9x - 32$

29) $y = -2x + 3$

30) $y = \frac{8}{3}x - \frac{25}{3}$

31) $y = -\frac{3}{4}x - \frac{7}{2}$

32) $y = \frac{1}{4}x - \frac{5}{4}$

Graphing Linear Inequalities

1)

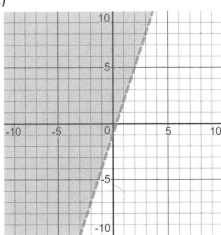

2)

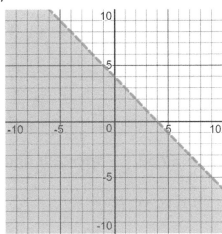

3)

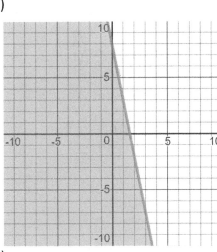

4)

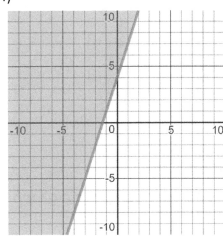

5)

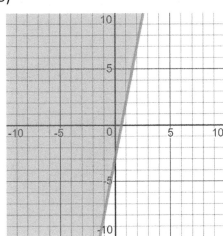

6)

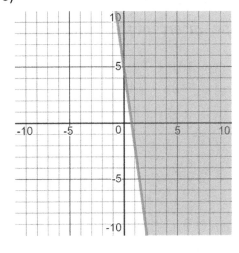

Slope and Rate of Change

1) undefined

2) $\dfrac{5}{6}$

3) $\dfrac{1}{2}$

4) 0

5) undefined

6) 0

7) -4

8) $\dfrac{-1}{7}$

9) 8

10) -4

11) -3

12) 2

Find the Slope, x – intercept and y–intercept

1) y intercept $= \dfrac{10}{7}$

   x intercept $= 10$

2) y intercept $= 3$

   x intercept $= -3$

3) y intercept $= -3$

   x intercept $= \dfrac{3}{2}$

4) y intercept $= \dfrac{5}{2}$

   x intercept $= \dfrac{5}{3}$

5) y intercept $= -\dfrac{7}{2}$

   x intercept $= \dfrac{7}{5}$

6) y intercept $= 4$

   x intercept $= -4$

Write an equation from a graph

1) $y = 2x - 4$

2) $y = 7x + 3$

3) $y = 9x$

4) $y = 7x + 5$

Slope–intercept form and Point–slope form

1) $y = 14x + 7$

2) $y = -2x - 14$

3) $y = -\dfrac{11}{7}x + 8$

4) $y = -\dfrac{9}{5}x - 7$

5) $y = \dfrac{x}{3} - 2$

6) $y = \dfrac{13}{11}x + \dfrac{12}{11}$

7) $y = \dfrac{11}{8}x + 6$

8) $y = \dfrac{3}{2}x + 8$

9) $y = -3x - 4$

10) $y = -2x + 5$

11) $y = -x - 2$

12) $y = -\dfrac{6}{5}x - 3$

13) $m = 2, (-3, 0)$

14) $m = \dfrac{2}{3}, (4, -2)$

15) $m = -\dfrac{3}{2}, (0, -3)$

16) $m = \dfrac{1}{2}, (3, 3)$

17) $m = \frac{13}{10}, (-1, -2)$

18) $m = 3, (0, 5)$

19) $m = -2, (4, 3)$

20) $m = 0, (3, -3)$

21) $m = 3, (-6, -2)$

22) $m = -4, (2, 7)$

23) $y - 2 = 7(x - 1)$

24) $y - 5 = \frac{5}{3}(x - 3) = 0$

25) $y + 4 = -(x - 2)$

26) $y - 2 = 2(x + 1)$

27) $y - 4 = 4(x + 1)$

28) $y - 2 = 2(x + 1)$

29) $y - 1 = \frac{1}{2}(x - 3)$

30) $y - 5 = -4(x + 2)$

Equations of horizontal and vertical lines

1)

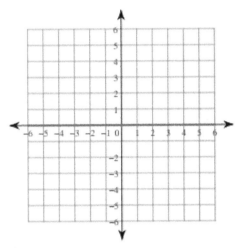

2)

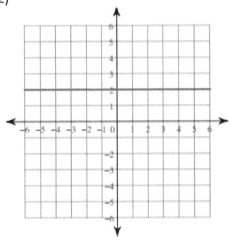

3)

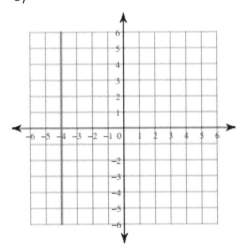

4)

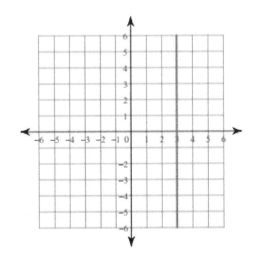

5)

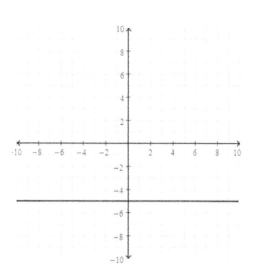

6)

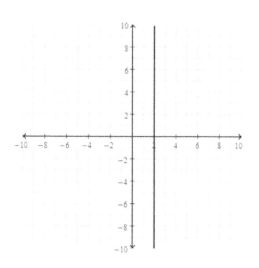

Equation of parallel or perpendicular lines

1) $y = -\frac{4}{7}x - \frac{36}{7}$

2) $y = -x - 2$

3) $y = 2x + 9$

4) $y = 3x + 30$

5) $y = -\frac{3}{5}x + 2$

6) $y = 6x + 1$

7) $y = \frac{1}{5}x - \frac{17}{5}$

8) $y = \frac{6}{5}x + \frac{14}{5}$

9) $y = -\frac{5}{2}x + \frac{9}{2}$

10) $y = -\frac{2}{3}x + \frac{1}{3}$

11) $y = 4x - 3$

12) $y = -\frac{6}{5}x + \frac{7}{5}$

13) $x = 2$

14) $y = 3$

15) $y = -8x + 3$

16) $y = \frac{1}{2}x + \frac{5}{2}$

17) $y = -\frac{9}{5}x - 4$

18) $y = -x + 3$

Graphing Absolute Value Equations

1) y = |x + 4|

2) y = |x − 1|

3) y = − |x| − 1

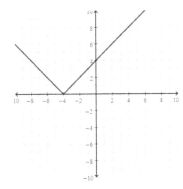

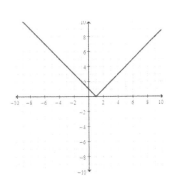

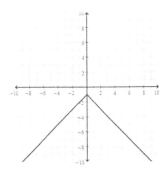

4) y = |x − 2|

5) y = − |x − 2|

6) y = −2 |2x + 2| + 4

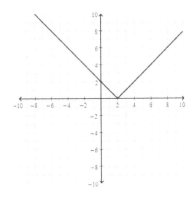

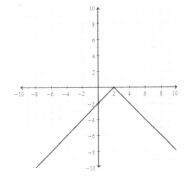

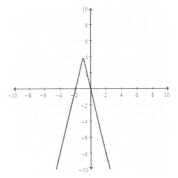

Chapter 4: Factoring

Topics that you'll learn in this chapter:

- ✓ GCF and LCM
- ✓ GCF of Monomials
- ✓ Factoring Quadratics
- ✓ Factoring by Grouping

Greatest Common Factor

✎ *Find the GCF for each number pair.*

1) 4, 2	9) 5, 12	17) 32, 24
2) 3, 5	10) 4, 14	18) 18, 36
3) 2, 6	11) 15, 18	19) 26, 20
4) 4, 7	12) 12, 20	20) 30, 14
5) 5, 10	13) 12, 16	21) 24, 20
6) 6, 12	14) 15, 27	22) 14, 22
7) 7, 14	15) 8, 24	23) 25, 15
8) 6, 14	16) 28, 16	24) 28, 32

Least Common Multiple

Find the LCM for each number pair.

1) 3, 6

2) 5, 10

3) 6, 14

4) 8, 9

5) 6, 18

6) 10, 12

7) 4, 12

8) 5, 15

9) 4, 18

10) 9, 12

11) 12, 16

12) 15, 18

13) 8, 24

14) 9, 28

15) 12, 24

16) 15, 20

17) 25, 18

18) 27, 24

19) 28, 18

20) 16, 30

21) 14, 28

22) 20, 35

23) 25, 30

24) 32, 27

GCF of Monomials

✎ *Find the GCF of each set of monomials.*

1) $39x, 30xy$

2) $60a, 56a^2$

3) $18x^2, 54x^2$

4) $36x^2, 21x^3$

5) $20a^2, 30a^2b$

6) $80a^3, 30a^2b$

7) $54x^3, 36x^3$

8) $33x, 44y^2x$

9) $15x^2, 12, 48$

10) $10v^3, 45v^3, 35v$

11) p^2q^2, pqr

12) $15m^2n, 25m^2n^2$

13) $12x^2yz, 3xy^2$

14) $22m^5n^2, 11m^2n^4$

15) $16x^3y, 8x^2$

16) $14ab^5, 7a^2b^2c$

17) $12t^7u^2, 18t^3u^7$

18) $18t, 48t^4$

19) $18r^3t, 26qr^2t^4$

20) $11a^4b^3, 44a^2b^5$

21) $16f, 21ab^2$

22) $12a^2b^2c^2, 20abc$

23) $18ab, 9ab$

24) $22m^5n^2, 11m^2n^4$

25) $4xy, 2x^2$

26) $x^3yz^2, 2x^3yz^3$

27) $140x, 140y^2, 80y^2$

28) $24a, 36a, 24ab^2$

29) $10x^3, 45x^3, 35x$

30) $105a, 30ab, 75a$

Factoring Quadratics

✎ *Factor each completely.*

1) $x^2 - 16x + 63 =$

2) $m^2 - 9m + 8 =$

3) $p^2 - 5p - 14 =$

4) $2b^2 + 17b + 21 =$

5) $a^2 + 5a + 4 =$

6) $a^2 + 2a - 15 =$

7) $4n^2 + 12n + 9 =$

8) $t^2 + 2t - 19 =$

9) $3x^3 + 21x^2 + 36x =$

10) $x^2 + 5x + 6 =$

11) $9r^2 - 5r - 10 =$

12) $30n^2b - 87nb + 30b =$

13) $7x^2 - 32x - 60 =$

14) $3b^3 - 5b^2 + 2b =$

15) $10m^2 + 89m - 9 =$

16) $4x^3 + 43x^2 + 30x =$

17) $9x^2 + 7 - 56 =$

18) $p^2 - 5p - 14 =$

19) $x^2 - 7x - 18 =$

20) $7x^2 - 31x - 20 =$

21) $6n^2 + 7n - 49 =$

22) $-6x^2 - 25x - 25 =$

23) $6x^2 + 5x - 6 =$

24) $16x^2 + 60x - 100 =$

25) $4x^2 - 35x + 49 =$

26) $5x^2 - 18x + 9 =$

27) $9n^2 + 66n + 21 =$

28) $3x^2 - 8x + 4 =$

29) $6x^2 - 36xy =$

30) $-6x^3 - 23x^2y - 10y^2x =$

31) $9a^2 + 9ab - 4b^2 =$

32) $4x^2 + 4xy - 35y^2 =$

33) $7x^2y - 27xy^2 + 18y^3 =$

34) $-2x^2 + 8xy + 64y^2 =$

35) $25mp^2 - 45mp =$

36) $14b^2 + 142b + 144 =$

37) $5x^2 + 85xy + 350y^2 =$

38) $7x^2 + 9xy =$

Factoring by Grouping

✎ *Factor each completely.*

1) $28xy - 7k - 49x + 4ky =$

2) $7xy - 3n - x + 21ny =$

3) $56n^3 + 64n^2 + 70n + 80 =$

4) $32u^2v - 12u^3m + 48u^4 - 8umv =$

5) $70n^4 + 40n^3 + 28n^2 + 16n =$

6) $45uv - 125bu - 75u^2 + 75bv =$

7) $x^3 + 7x^2 + 6x + 42 =$

8) $6x^3 + 36x^2 + 30x + 180 =$

9) $6m^3 - 30m^2 + 30m - 150 =$

10) $2x^3 - 4x^2 - 10x + 20 =$

11) $24p^3 + 15p^2 - 56p - 35 =$

12) $42mc + 36md - 7n^2c - 6n^2d =$

13) $28x^4 + 112x^2 - 21x^2 - 84x =$

14) $15xw + 18xk + 25yw + 30k =$

15) $56xy - 35x + 16ry - 10r =$

16) $4xy + 6 - x - 24y =$

17) $192x3 + 72x2 + 144x + 54 =$

18) $8x3 - 8x2 + 14x - 14 =$

19) $20x^3 + 5x^2 + 28x + 7 =$

20) $100x^3 + 160x^2 - 60x - 96 =$

Answers of Worksheets – Chapter 4

Greatest Common Factor

1) 2	9) 1	17) 8
2) 1	10) 2	18) 18
3) 2	11) 3	19) 2
4) 1	12) 4	20) 2
5) 5	13) 4	21) 4
6) 6	14) 3	22) 2
7) 7	15) 8	23) 5
8) 2	16) 4	24) 4

Least Common Multiple

2) 6	10) 36	18) 450
3) 10	11) 36	19) 216
4) 42	12) 48	20) 252
5) 72	13) 90	21) 240
6) 18	14) 24	22) 28
7) 60	15) 252	23) 140
8) 12	16) 24	24) 150
9) 15	17) 60	25) 864

GCF of Monomials

1) $3x$	11) pq	21) no
2) 4	12) $5m^2n$	22) $4abc$
3) $18x^2$	13) $3xy$	23) $9ab$
4) $3x^2$	14) $11m^2n$	24) $11m^2n^2$
5) $10a^2$	15) $8x^2$	25) $2x$
6) $10a^2$	16) $7ab^2$	26) x^3yz^2
7) $18x^3$	17) $6t^3u^2$	27) 20
8) $11x$	18) $8t$	28) $12a$
9) 3	19) $2r^2t$	29) $5x$
10) $5v$	20) $11a^2b^3$	30) $15a$

Factoring Quadratics

1) $(x - 9)(x - 7)$
2) $(m - 1)(m - 8)$
3) $(p + 2)(p - 7)$
4) $(2b + 3)(b + 7)$
5) $a^2 + 5a + 4$
6) $a^2 + 2a - 15$
7) $4n^2 + 12n + 9$
8) $t^2 + 2t - 19$
9) $3x^3 + 21x^2 + 36x$
10) $x^2 + 5x + 6$
11) $9r^2 - 5r - 10$
12) $30n^2b\ 87nb + 30b$
13) $7x^2 - 32x - 60$
14) $3b^3 - 5b^2 + 2b$
15) $10m^2 + 89m - 9$
16) $4x^3 + 43x^2 + 30x$
17) $9x^2 + 7x - 56$
18) $p^2 - 5p - 14$
19) $x^2 - 7x - 18$
20) $7x^2 - 31x - 20$
21) $(3n - 7)(2x + 7)$
22) $-(2x + 5)(3x + 5)$

23) $(2x + 3)(3x - 2)$
24) $4(x + 5)(4x - 5)$
25) $(x - 7)(4x - 7)$
26) $(5x - 3)(x - 3)$
27) $3(3n + 1)(n + 7)$
28) $(3x - 2)(x - 2)$
29) $6x(x - 6y)$
30) $-x(2x + y)(3x + 10y)$
31) $(3a + 4b)(3a - b)$
32) $(2x + 7y)(2x - 5y)$
33) $y(7x - 6y)(x - 3y)$
34) $-2(x - 8y)(x + 4y)$
35) $5mp(5p - 9)$
36) $2(7b + 8)(b + 9)$
37) $5(x + 10y)(x + 7y)$
38) $x(7x + 9y)$

Factoring by Grouping

1) $(7x + k)(4y - 7)$
2) $(x + 3n)(7y - 1)$
3) $2(4n^2 + 5)(7n + 8)$
4) $4u(4u - m)(2v + 3u^2)$
5) $2n(5n^2 + 2)(7n + 4)$
6) $5(3u + 5b)(3v - 5u)$
7) $(x^2 + 6)(x + 7)$
8) $6(x^2 + 5)(x + 6)$
9) $6(m^2 + 5)(m - 5)$
10) $2(x^2 - 5)(x - 2)$

11) $(3p^2 - 7)(8p + 5)$
12) $(6m - n^2)(7c + 6d)$
13) $7x(4x^2 - 3)(x + 4)$
14) $(3x + 5y)(5w + 6k)$
15) $(7x + 2r)(8y - 5)$
16) $(x - 6)(4y - 1)$
17) $(4x^2 + 1)(3x - 5)$
18) $2(4x^2 + 7)(x - 1)$
19) $(5x^2 + 7)(4x + 1)$
20) $4(5x^2 - 3)(5x + 8)$

Chapter 5: Inequalities and System of Equations

Topics that you'll learn in this chapter:

- ✓ One–Step Inequalities
- ✓ Two–Step Linear Inequalities
- ✓ Advanced Linear Inequalities
- ✓ Compound Inequalities
- ✓ Absolute Value Inequalities
- ✓ Systems of Equations
- ✓ Systems of Equations Word Problems

One–Step Inequalities

✎ *Solve inequalities.*

1) $x + 8 \geq 18$

2) $v - 1 < 3$

3) $r + 13 < 9$

4) $n - 2 \leq 4$

5) $p + 8 > -4$

6) $17 + k \leq 10$

7) $x + 13 \geq 5$

8) $x - 12 < 11$

9) $x - 5 \leq 8$

10) $x - 1 \geq 2$

11) $9x > -54$

12) $4x \leq 12$

13) $x + 4 < 2$

14) $x + 2 > 7$

15) $-11 < -9 + y$

16) $7 \geq x - 5$

17) $-4 + k < 19$

18) $-9 + a > 8$

19) $12 > c + 5$

20) $1 + q > -10$

✎ *Graph each inequality.*

21) $6x > -24$

22) $-2 < \dfrac{x}{4}$

23) $\dfrac{x}{3} > 2$

24) $4x < 8$

25) $12 < 3x$

26) $\dfrac{x}{3} < 1$

Two–Step Linear Inequalities

✎ *Solve each inequality and graph its solution.*

1) $84 \geq -7(v-9)$

2) $-4x-5 > -25$

3) $7n-1 > -169$

4) $132 > 12(n+9)$

5) $-11x-4 > -15$

6) $-3(p-7) \geq 21$

7) $-4(3+n) > -32$

8) $-3(p+1) \leq -18$

9) $-3(r-4) \geq 0$

10) $-b-2 > 8$

11) $2x+4 \geq 24$

12) $8x+2 \leq 138$

13) $4 > \frac{a+1}{2}$

14) $\frac{x+1}{2} \geq -4$

15) $-18 + \frac{k}{3} \leq -26$

16) $\frac{n+3}{2} > -2$

17) $-2 + \frac{x}{2} > 6$

18) $\frac{1+m}{9} \geq 1$

✎ *Write the inequality for each graph.*

19) $x + 2 \leq -7$

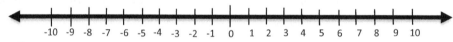

20) $-5 < -5 + \frac{x}{2}$

21) $5x + 8 \geq -2$

22) $12x - 9 > 27$

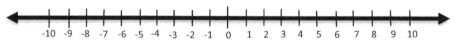

23) $21 < -4x + 5$

24) $5 + \frac{x}{3} < 8$

Advanced Linear Inequalities

✍ *Sketch the graph of each linear inequality.*

1) $y \geq -5x + 2$

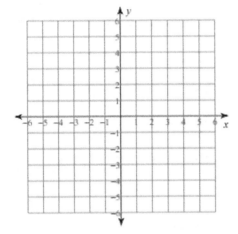

2) $x < -3$

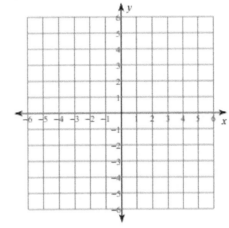

3) $6x - 3y < 12$

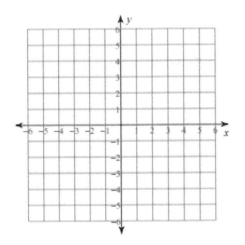

4) $7x - 5y \leq -15$

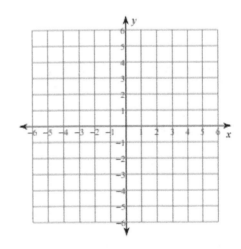

Solve Compound Inequalities

✍ **Solve each inequality.**

1) $8 \geq 2x > -10$

2) $-14 < -11 + x \leq -12$

3) $x + 11 > 9$ or $8x \geq -24$

4) $x + 9 > 6$ or $x - 1 \leq -10$

5) $x + 2 \leq -3$ or $x - 5 > -2$

6) $-15 \leq x - 13 \leq 0$

7) $20x > 40$ or $\dfrac{x}{7} > 2$

8) $-11 < \dfrac{x}{3} < -9$

9) $\dfrac{x}{6} \leq 4$ and $x - 22 > -23$

10) $x - 2 \leq 3$ and $\dfrac{x}{7} > -5$

11) $y - 6 \leq -7$ or $y + 3 \geq 7$

12) $27 < 3a < 39$

13) $5n \geq 5$ and $n + 2 \leq 9$

14) $x - 5 < -1$ or $x + 6 > 14$

15) $-4 < x + 11 < 2$

16) $8x \leq 32$ or $6x \geq 72$

17) $10 > x > -8$

18) $\dfrac{x}{2} \leq 1$ or $x + 9 > 14$

✍ **Solve each compound inequality and graph its solution.**

19) $x - 5 < -9$ or $\dfrac{x}{5} > 3$

20) $-4 < 12 + a < 22$

21) $12n < 24$ or $\dfrac{n}{9} \geq 13$

22) $x + 9 \geq 15$ and $\dfrac{x}{6} \leq 4$

23) $-8 \leq \dfrac{m}{2} < 5$

24) $r + 6 \geq 19$ or $\dfrac{r}{3} < -6$

Solve Absolute Value Inequalities

✎ **Solve each inequality and graph its solution.**

1) $\left|\frac{x}{8}\right| \leq 6$

2) $|-14n| \leq 34$

3) $\left|\frac{x}{5}\right| \geq 5$

4) $|-3b| \leq 42$

5) $|-6n| < 48$

6) $|x + 8| < 11$

7) $|3m - 6| \leq 33$

8) $|6 + 9x| < 14$

9) $|3 - 9a| \leq 60$

10) $|7x + 8| \geq 22$

11) $\left|\frac{x-4}{5}\right| \geq 2$

12) $\left|\frac{3+r}{7}\right| \geq 8$

✎ **Solve each inequality and graph its solution.**

1) $|x| - 11 > -14$

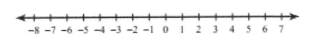

2) $|n| - 9 \leq -7$

3) $|a| + 7 < 23$

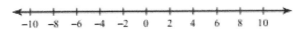

4) $|x| + 6 > 32$

5) $|x| - 11 \leq 0$

6) $|z| + 5 < 13$

7) $|x - 8| + 8 > 13$

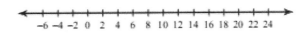

8) $-5 + |n - 9| > 23$

Systems of Equations

✎ *Solve each system of equations.*

1) $-2x + 2y = 4$ $x =$ ___

     $-2x + y = 3$ $y =$ ___

2) $-10x + 2y = -6$ $x =$ ___

     $6x - 16y = 48$ $y =$ ___

3) $y = -8$ $x =$ ___

     $16x - 12y = 32$

4) $2y = -6x + 10$ $x =$ ___

     $10x - 8y = -6$ $y =$ ___

5) $10x - 9y = -13$ $x =$ ___

     $-5x + 3y = 11$ $y =$ ___

6) $-3x - 4y = 5$ $x =$ ___

     $x - 2y = 5$ $y =$ ___

7) $5x - 14y = -23$ $x =$ ___

     $-6x + 7y = 8$ $y =$ ___

8) $10x - 14y = -4$ $x =$ ___

     $-10x - 20y = -30$ $y =$ ___

9) $-4x + 12y = 12$ $x =$ ___

     $-14x + 16y = -10$ $y =$ ___

10) $x + 20y = 56$ $x =$ ___

     $x + 15y = 41$ $y =$ ___

11) $6x - 7y = -8$ $x =$ ___

     $-x - 4y = -9$ $y =$ ___

12) $-3x + 2y = -18$ $x =$ ___

     $8x - 2y = 28$ $y =$ ___

13) $-5x + y = -3$ $x =$ ___

     $3x - 8y = 24$ $y =$ ___

14) $3x - 2y = 2$ $x =$ ___

     $5x - 5y = 10$ $y =$ ___

15) $8x + 14y = 4$ $x =$ ___

     $-6x - 7y = -10$ $y =$ ___

16) $10x + 7y = 1$ $x =$ ___

     $-5x - 7y = 24$ $y =$ ___

Systems of Equations Word Problems

✎ *Solve each word problem.*

1) Tickets to a movie cost $5 for adults and $3 for students. A group of friends purchased 18 tickets for $82.00. How many adults ticket did they buy? _____

2) At a store, Eva bought two shirts and five hats for $154.00. Nicole bought three same shirts and four same hats for $168.00. What is the price of each shirt? _____

3) A farmhouse shelters 10 animals, some are pigs, and some are ducks. Altogether there are 36 legs. How many pigs are there? _____

4) A class of 195 students went on a field trip. They took 19 vehicles, some cars and some buses. If each car holds 5 students and each bus hold 25 students, how many buses did they take? _____

5) A theater is selling tickets for a performance. Mr. Smith purchased 8 senior tickets and 5 child tickets for $136 for his friends and family. Mr. Jackson purchased 4 senior tickets and 6 child tickets for $96. What is the price of a senior ticket? $_____

6) The difference of two numbers is 6. Their sum is 14. What is the bigger number? $_____

7) The sum of the digits of a certain two-digit number is 7. Reversing its digits increase the number by 9. What is the number? _____

8) The difference of two numbers is 18. Their sum is 66. What are the numbers? _____

9) The length of a rectangle is 3 meters greater than 2 times the width. The perimeter of rectangle is 30 meters. What is the length of the rectangle? _____

10) Jim has 44 nickels and dimes totaling $2.95. How many nickels does he have? _____

Answers of Worksheets – Chapter 5

One–Step Inequalities

1) $x \geq 10$

2) $v < 4$

3) $r < -4$

4) $n \leq 6$

5) $p > -12$

6) $k \leq -7$

7) $x \geq -8$

8) $x23$

9) $x \leq 13$

10) $x \geq 3$

11) $x > -6$

12) $x \leq 3$

13) $x < -2$

14) $x > 5$

15) $-2 < y$

16) $12 \geq x$

17) $k < 23$

18) $a > 17$

19) $7 > c$

20) $q > -11$

21)

22)

23)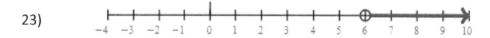

24)

25)

26)

Two–Step Linear Inequalities

1) $3 \geq v$

2) $x > 5$

3) $n > 24$

4) $2 > n$

5) $x > 1$

6) $p \geq 0$

7) $n > 5$

8) $p \leq 5$

9) $r \geq 4$

10) $b > -10$ 13) $7 > a$ 16) $n > -7$

11) $x \geq 10$ 14) $x \geq -9$ 17) $x > 16$

12) $x \leq 17$ 15) $k \leq -24$ 18) $m \geq 8$

19)

20)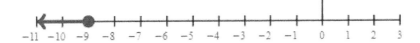

21)

22)

23)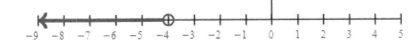

24)

Advanced Linear Inequalities

1)

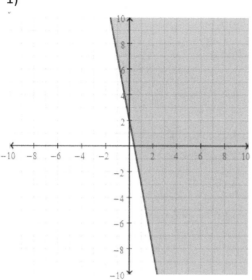

2)

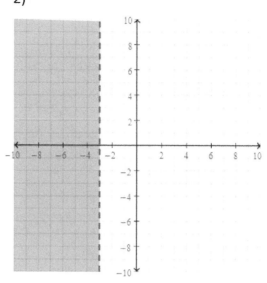

3)

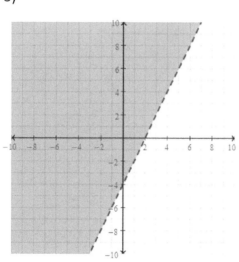

4)

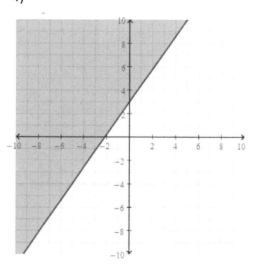

Compound Inequalities

1) $4 \geq x > -5$

2) $-3 < x \leq -1$

3) $x > -2 \ or \ x \geq -3$

4) $x > -3 \ or \ x \leq -9$

5) $x \leq -5 \ or \ x > 3$

6) $-2 \leq x \leq 13$

7) $x > 2$ *or* $x > 14$

8) $-33 < x < -27$

9) $x \leq 24$ *and* $x > -1$

10) $x - 2 \leq 3$ *and* $\frac{x}{7} > -5$

11) $y - 6 \leq -7$ *or* $y + 3 \geq 7$

12) $27 < 3a < 39$

13) $5n \geq 5$ *and* $n + 2 \leq 9$

14) $x - 5 < -1$ *or* $x + 6 > 14$

15) $-4 < x + 11 < 2$

16) $8x \leq 32$ *or* $6x \geq 72$

17) $10 > x > -8$

18) $\frac{x}{2} \leq 1$ *or* $x + 9 > 14$

19)

20)

21)

22)

23)

24)

Absolute Value Inequalities

1) $x \leq 48$ *and* $x \geq -48$

2) $n \geq \frac{-17}{7}$ *and* $n \leq \frac{17}{7}$

3) $x \geq 25$ *or* $x \leq -25$

4) $x \geq -14$ *or* $x \leq 14$

5) $n > -8$ *and* $n < 8$

6) $x < 3$ *and* $x > -19$

7) $m \leq 13$ *and* $m \geq -9$

8) $x < \frac{4}{3}$ *and* $x > \frac{-16}{9}$

9) $a \geq \frac{-19}{3}$ and $a \leq 7$

11) $-6 \leq x \leq 14$

10) $x \geq 2$ or $x \leq -\frac{30}{7}$

12) $r \geq 53$ or $r \leq -59$

13)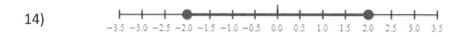

14)

15)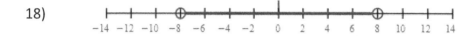

16)

17)

18)

19)

20)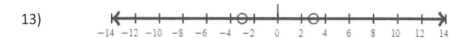

Systems of Equations

1) $x = -1, y = 1$

2) $x = 0, y = -3$

3) $x = -4$

4) $x = 1, y = 2$

5) $x = -4, y = -3$

6) $x = 1, y = -2$

7) $x = 1, y = 2$

8) $x = 1, y = 1$

9) $x = 3, y = 2$

10) $x = -4, y = 3$

11) $x = 1, y = 2$

12) $x = 2, y = -6$

13) $x = 0, y = -3$

14) $x = -2, y = -4$

15) $x = 4, y = -2$

16) $x = 5, y = -7$

Systems of Equations Word Problems

1) 14

2) $32

3) 8

4) 5

5) $12

6) 10

7) 34

8) 42, 24

9) 11 *meters*

10) 29

Chapter 6: Monomials Operations

Topics that you'll learn in this chapter:

- ✓ Add and Subtract Monomials
- ✓ Multiply and Divide Monomials
- ✓ GCF and Powers of Monomials
- ✓ Scientific Notation

Add and Subtract Monomials

✍ *Find each sum and difference.*

1) $5u^2v + 6u^2v$

2) $xyz + (-6xyz)$

3) $10u + (-2u)$

4) $12xy + xy$

5) $15y - 12y$

6) $(-5x) + (-7x)$

7) $(-40x) - 14x$

8) $56x^2 + 31x^2$

9) $y^4 - (-6y^4)$

10) $25x^3 + 75x^3$

11) $5xy^2z + (-7xy^2z)$

12) $5x^2yz^2 + 8x^2yz^2$

13) $6y^6 - (-15y^6)$

14) $2x^2 - (-8x^2)$

15) $(-6pqr) + 3pqr$

16) $8x^4y - 6x^4y$

17) $18r^2\,t^4 + 26r^2t^4$

18) $51x^2yz^2 - 21x^2yz^2$

Multiply and Divide Monomials

✏️**Find each product.**

1) $2xy^2z \times 4z^2$

2) $4xy \times x^2y$

3) $4pq^3 \times (-2p^4q)$

4) $8s^4t^2 \times st^5$

5) $12p^3 \times (-3p^4)$

6) $-4p^2q^3r \times 6pq^2r^3$

7) $(-8a^4) \times (-12a^6b)$

8) $3u^4v^2 \times (-7u^2v^3)$

9) $4u^3 \times (-2u)$

10) $-6xy^2 \times 3x^2y$

11) $12y^2z^3 \times (-y^2z)$

12) $5a^2bc^2 \times 2abc^2$

✏️ **Solve.**

13) $\dfrac{r^4t^3}{r^5\,t^7}$

14) $\dfrac{12x^8}{3x^5}$

15) $\dfrac{x^8y^6}{x^7y^2}$

16) $\dfrac{48x^3y^5z^6}{-8xyz^2}$

17) $\dfrac{-8x^6y^2}{2x^3y^2}$

18) $\dfrac{4ab^{-2}}{-3c^{-2}} =$

19) $\left(\dfrac{3a}{2c}\right)^{-2} =$

20) $\left(-\dfrac{5x}{3yz}\right)^{-3} =$

21) $\dfrac{4ab^{-2}}{-3c^{-2}} =$

22) $\left(-\dfrac{x^3}{x^4}\right)^{-2} =$

23) $\left(-\dfrac{x^{-2}}{3x^2}\right)^{-3} =$

GCF and Powers of Monomials

✍ **Find the GCF of each pairs of expressions.**

1) $54x^3$, $36x^3$

2) 2) $33x$, $44y^2x$

3) $15x^2$, 12, 48

4) 4) $10v^3$, $45v^3$, $35v$

5) p^2q^2, pqr

6) 6) $15m^2n$, $25m^2n^2$

7) $12x^2yz$, $3xy^2$

8) 8) $22m^5n^2$, $11m^2n^4$

9) $16x^3y$, $8x^2$

10) 10) $14ab^5$, $7a^2b^2c$

11) $12t^7u^2$, $18t^3u^7$

12) 12) $18t$, $48t^4$

13) $18r^3t$, $26qr^2t^4$

14) 14) $11a^4b^3$, $44a^2b^5$

15) $16f$, $21ab^2$

16) 16) $12a^2b^2c^2$, $20abc$

17) $18ab$, $9ab$

18) 18) $22m^5n^2$, $11m^2n^4$

19) $4xy$, $2x^2$

20) 20) x^3yz^2, $2x^3yz^3$

✍ **Simplify.**

21) $(3x^4)^7$

22) $(4y^22y^3y)^2$

23) $(3x^2\,2x^2)^3$

24) $(8x^4y^3)^6$

25) $(3y^25y^2)^2$

26) $(6x^3y)^3$

27) $(8x^2x^23n)^2$

28) $(7xy^6)^3$

29) $(9x^3y^2)^4$

30) $(10y^3y^2)^3$

31) $(6x^2x^6)^3$

32) $(3x^74x^{\,3}k^2)^2$

33) $(4y^54y^2)^2$

34) $(5x2x^3)^3$

35) $(4y^3)^3$

36) $(y^3y^3y^2)^3$

37) $(4y^2y)^3$

38) $(6xy^6)^3$

Answers of Worksheets – Chapter 6

Add and Subtract monomials

1) $11u^2v$

2) $-5xyz$

3) $8u$

4) $13xy$

5) $13y$

6) $-12x$

7) $-54x$

8) $87x^2$

9) $7y^4$

10) $100x^3$

11) $-2xy^2z$

12) $13x^2yz^2$

13) $21y^6$

14) $10x^2$

15) $-3pqr$

16) $-6x^2y^4z^4$

17) $-4x^3$

18) $-6x^2y^4z^4$

19) $-6x^2y^4z^4$

20) $-6x^2y^4z^4$

21) $-6x^2y^4z^4$

22) $-6x^2y^4z^4$

Multiply and Divide monomials

1) $8xy^2z^3$

2) $4x^3y^2$

3) $-8p^5q^4$

4) $8s^5t^7$

5) $-36p^7$

6) $-24p^3q^5r^4$

7) $96a^{10}b$

8) $-21u^6v^5$

9) $-8u^4$

10) $-18x3y3$

11) $-12y4z4$

12) $10a3b2c4$

13) $\frac{1}{r\,t^4}$

14) $4x^3$

15) xy^4

16) $-6x^2z4$

17) $-4x3$

18) $-\frac{4ac^2}{3b^2}$

19) $\frac{4c^2}{9a^2}$

20) $-\frac{27y^3z^3}{125x^3}$

21) $-\frac{4ac^2}{3b^2}$

22) x^2

23) $-81x^{12}$

GCF and Powers of monomials

1) $10x^2$

2) 4

3) 10

4) 7xy

5) 6y7x

6) 3x

7) 3

8) $7xy^2$

9) $18x^2$

10) $(15)x$

11) 27

12) 3

13) $20x$

14) $2x^2y$

15) xy

16) $2x^2y^2$

17) $6xy^4$

18) $5x^3y$

19) $2187x^{28}$

20) $72x^{12}$

21) $216x^{12}$

22) $262144x^{24}y^{18}$

23) $225y^{10}$

24) $216x^9y^3$

25) $576x^8n^2$

26) $343x^3y^{18}$

27) $6561x^{12}y^8$

28) $1000y^{15}$

29) $396x^{24}$

30) $144x^{100}k^4$

31) $256y^{14}$

32) $1000x^{12}$

33) $64y^9$

34) $27y^{18}$

35) $64y^9$

36) $216x^3y^{18}$

Chapter 7: Quadratic

Topics that you'll learn in this chapter:

- ✓ Quadratic Equations
- ✓ Graphing Quadratic Functions
- ✓ Quadratic Equations
- ✓ Solve a Quadratic Equation by Factoring
- ✓ Quadratic Equation and Transformations of Quadratic Functions
- ✓ Quadratic Formula and the Discriminant

Quadratic Equation

✍ *Multiply.*

1) $(x - 2)(x + 4) =$ _____

2) $(x + 1)(x + 6) =$ _____

3) $(x - 4)(x + 2) =$ _____

4) $(x + 5)(x - 3) =$ _____

5) $(x - 6)(x - 2) =$ _____

6) $(2x + 1)(x - 3) =$ _____

7) $(2x - 1)(x + 4) =$ _____

8) $(2x - 3)(x + 4) =$ _____

9) $(3x + 5)(x - 3) =$ _____

10) $(3x + 4)(2x - 2) =$ _____

✍ *Factor each expression.*

11) $x^2 - 5x + 4 =$ _____

12) $x^2 + 6x + 8 =$ _____

13) $x^2 + x - 12 =$ _____

14) $x^2 - 7x + 10 =$ _____

15) $x^2 - 4x - 12 =$ _____

16) $2x^2 - 3x - 2 =$ _____

17) $2x^2 + 8x + 8 =$ _____

18) $3x^2 - 14x + 5 =$ _____

19) $3x^2 + 4x + 1 =$ _____

20) $4x^2 - 12x + 8 =$ _____

✍ *Solve each equation.*

21) $(x + 2)(x - 4) = 0$

22) $(x + 5)(x + 8) = 0$

23) $(2x + 4)(x + 3) = 0$

24) $(3x - 9)(2x + 6) = 0$

25) $x^2 - 11x + 19 = -5$

26) $x^2 + 7x + 18 = 8$

27) $x^2 - 10x + 22 = -2$

28) $x^2 + 3x - 12 = 6$

29) $5x^2 - 5x - 10 = 0$

30) $6x^2 - 6x = 36$

Graphing Quadratic Functions

✍ *Sketch the graph of each function. Identify the vertex and axis of symmetry.*

1) $y = 3(x + 1)^2 + 2$

2) $y = -(x - 2)^2 - 4$

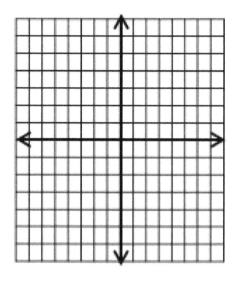

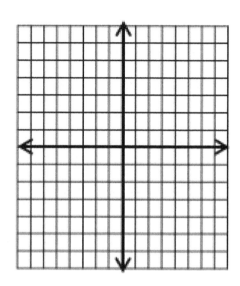

3) $y = 2(x - 3)^2 + 8$

4) $y = x^2 - 8x + 19$

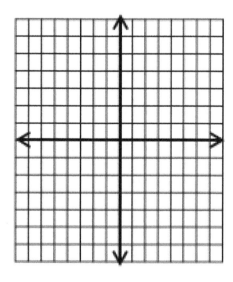

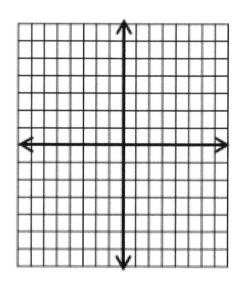

Quadratic Equations

✍ Factor each completely.

1) $18n^2 - 180$

2) $16z^2 - 1$

3) $49x^2 - 25y^2$

4) $25a^2 + 16b^2$

5) $4x^2 + 49y^2$

6) $54a^2 - 6b^2$

7) $2x^4r - 72y^4r$

8) $4x^4 - 144y^4$

9) $7a^4 - 28b^4$

10) $216x^4yz - 6z^5y$

11) $150x^2 - 216$

12) $20x^2 - 45$

13) $x^2 - 36$

14) $16m^6 - n^6$

✍ Solve each equation by factoring.

15) $x^2 - \frac{18}{27}0$

16) $\frac{32}{64} - b^2 = 0$

17) $22a^2 = 44$

18) $32 - 162x^2 = 0$

19) $81y^2 = 9$

20) $36x^2 - 64 = 0$

21) $42a^2 = 56a$

22) $84x^2 = 156$

✍ Solve each equation by completing the square

23) $x^2 + 9x - 36 = 0$

24) $a^2 - 12a + 36 = 0$

25) $x^2 + 12x - 45 = 0$

26) $18x^2 + 24x - 24 = 0$

27) $y^2 - 17y + 30 = 0$

28) $x^2 - 9x - 22 = 0$

29) $a^2 - 13a + 40 = 0$

30) $8n^2 - 4n - 84 = 0$

31) $x^2 - 5x - 28 = 0$

32) $a^2 - a = 6$

33) $x^2 + x - 30 = 0$

34) $35 = x^2 - 2x$

35) $7a = a^2 + 12$

36) $x^2 - 5x + 4 = 0$

37) $a^2 - 6a - 16 = 0$

38) $n^2 - 6n - 27 = 0$

Solve a Quadratic Equation by Factoring

✎ **Solve each equation by factoring or using the quadratic formula.**

1) $(x + 2)(x - 7) = 0$

2) $(x + 3)(x + 5) = 0$

3) $(x - 9)(x + 4) = 0$

4) $(x - 7)(x - 5) = 0$

5) $(x + 4)(x + 8) = 0$

6) $(5x + 7)(x + 4) = 0$

7) $(2x + 5)(4x + 3) = 0$

8) $(3x + 4)(x + 2) = 0$

9) $(6x + 3)(2x + 4) = 0$

10) $(9x + 3)(x + 6) = 0$

11) $x^2 = 2x$

12) $x^2 - 6 = x$

13) $2x^2 + 4 = 6x$

14) $-x^2 - 6 = 5x$

15) $x^2 + 8x = 9$

16) $x^2 + 10x = 24$

17) $x^2 + 7x = -10$

18) $x^2 + 12x = -32$

19) $x^2 + 11x = -28$

20) $x^2 + x - 20 = 2x$

21) $x^2 + 8x = -15$

22) $7x^2 - 14x = -7$

23) $10x^2 = 27x - 18$

24) $7x^2 - 6x + 3 = 3$

25) $2x^2 - 14 = -3x$

26) $10x^2 - 26x = -12$

27) $15x^2 + 80 = -80x$

28) $x^2 + 15x = -56$

29) $6x^2 - 18x - 18 = 6$

30) $2x^2 + 6x - 24 = 12$

31) $2x^2 - 22x + 38 = -10$

32) $-4x^2 - 8x - 3 = -3 - 5x^2$

Quadratic Formula and Transformations of Quadratic Functions

✎ **Solve the quadratic equations using quadratic formula.**

1) $x^2 + 2x - 8 = 0$
2) $x^2\ 5x - 6 = 0$
3) $2x^2 - 5x + 3 = 0$
4) $2x^2 - x - 13 = 2$
5) $2x^2 - x - 4 = 2$
6) $x^2 - 4x - 14 = -2$
7) $8x^2 - 4x = 18$

8) $8x^2 + 6x = -5$
9) $10x^2 + 9 = x$
10) $x^2 = 9x - 20$
11) $9x^2 - 11 = 6x$
12) $4x^2 - 8 = a$
13) $14x^2 + 1 = 6x^2 + 7x$
14) $4x^2 + 4x - 8 = 1$

✎ **State the transformations and sketch the graph of each function.**

15) $y - 2 = (x - 4)^2$

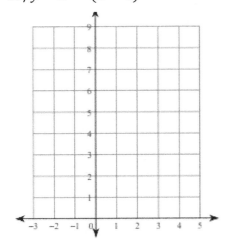

16) $y - 5 = (x - 2)^2$

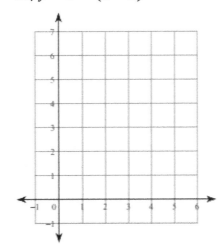

17) $y + 7 = (x + 3)^2$

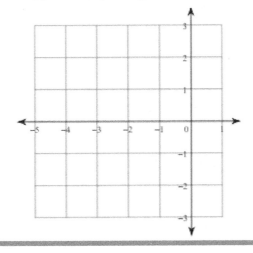

18) $y + 9 = (x - 1)^2$

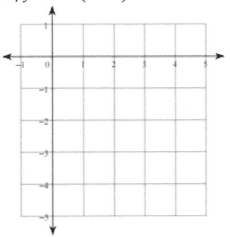

Quadratic Formula and the Discriminant

✍ **Find the value of the discriminant of each quadratic equation.**

1) $x(x - 1) = 0$

2) $x^2 + 2x - 1 = 0$

3) $x^2 + 3x + 5 = 0$

4) $x^2 - x + 4 = 0$

5) $x^2 + x - 2 = 0$

6) $x^2 + 4x - 6 = 0$

7) $x^2 + 5x + 2 = 0$

8) $2x^2 - 2x - 7 = 0$

9) $2x^2 + 3x + 9 = 0$

10) $2x^2 + 5x - 4 = 0$

11) $5x^2 + x - 2 = 0$

12) $-3x^2 - 6x + 2 = 0$

13) $-4x^2 - 4x + 5 = 0$

14) $-2x^2 - x - 1 = 0$

15) $6x^2 - 2x - 3 = 0$

16) $-5x^2 - 3x + 9 = 0$

17) $4x^2 + 5x - 4 = 0$

18) $8x^2 - 9x = 0$

19) $3x^2 - 5x + 1 = 0$

20) $5x^2 + 6x + 4 = 0$

✍ **Find the discriminant of each quadratic equation then state the number of real and imaginary solutions.**

21) $-x^2 - 9 = 6x$

22) $4x^2 = 8x - 4$

23) $-4x^2 - 4x = 6$

24) $8x^2 - 6x + 3 = 5x^2$

25) $-9x^2 = -8x + 8$

26) $9x^2 + 6x + 6 = 5$

27) $9x^2 - 3x - 8 = -10$

28) $-2x^2 - 8x - 14 = -6$

Answers of Worksheets – Chapter 7

Quadratic equations

1) $x^2 + 2x - 8$
2) $x^2 + 7x + 6$
3) $x^2 - 2x - 8$
4) $x^2 + 2x - 15$
5) $x^2 - 8x + 12$
6) $2x^2 - 5x - 3$
7) $2x^2 + 7x - 4$
8) $2x^2 + 5x - 12$
9) $3x^2 - 4x - 15$
10) $6x^2 + 2x - 8$

11) $(x - 4)(x - 1)$
12) $(x + 4)(x + 2)$
13) $(x - 3)(x + 4)$
14) $(x - 5)(x - 2)$
15) $(x + 2)(x - 6)$
16) $(2x + 1)(x - 2)$
17) $(2x + 4)(x + 2)$
18) $(3x - 1)(x + 5)$
19) $(3x + 1)(x + 1)$
20) $(2x - 2)(2x - 4)$

21) $x = -2, x = 4$
22) $x = -5, x = -8$
23) $x = -2, x = -3$
24) $x = 3, x = -3$
25) $x = 3, x = 8$
26) $x = -2, x = -5$
27) $x = 4, x = 6$
28) $x = 3, x = -6$
29) $x = 2, x = -1$
30) $x = -2, x = 3$

Graphing quadratic functions

1) $(-1, 2), x = -1$

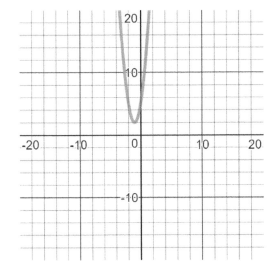

2) $(2, -4), x = 2$

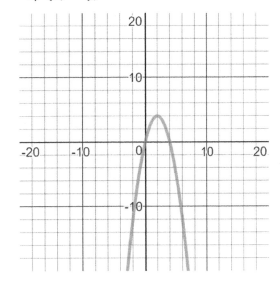

3) $(3, 8), x = 3$

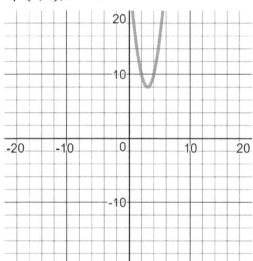

4) $(4, 3), x = 4$

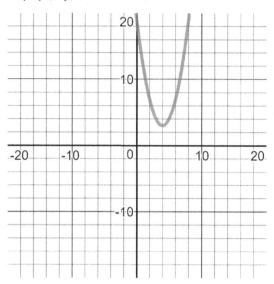

Quadratic equations

1) $18(n^2 - 10)$

2) $(4z + 1)(4z - 1)$

3) $(7x + 5y)(7x - 5y)$

4) *no*

5) *no*

6) $6(3v + u)(3v - u)$

7) $2r(x^2 + 6y^2)(x^2 - 6y^2)$

8) $4(x^2 + 6y^2)(x^2 - 6y^2)$

9) $7(x^2 + 2y^2)(x^2 - 2y^2)$

10) $6ay(6x^2 + y^2)(6x^2 - y^2)$

11) $6(5k + 6)(5k - 6)$

12) $5(2x + 3)(2x - 3)$

13) $(x + 6)(x - 6)$

14) $(4m^3 + n^3)(4m^3 - n^3)$

15) $(0.82, -0.82)$

16) $(-\frac{1}{2}\sqrt{2}, \frac{1}{2}\sqrt{2})$

17) $(\sqrt{2}, -\sqrt{2})$

18) $(-\frac{4}{9}, \frac{4}{9})$

19) $(\frac{1}{3}, -\frac{1}{3})$

20) $(\frac{4}{3}, -\frac{4}{3})$

21) $(\frac{4}{3}, 0)$

22) $(\frac{13}{7}, 0)$

23) $x = \{-4, -5\}$

24) $a = \{-6, -6\}$

25) $x = \{3, -15\}$

26) $x = \{\frac{2}{3}, -2\}$

27) $y = \{15, 2\}$

28) $x = \{-2, 11\}$

29) $a = \{8, 5\}$

30) $n = \{-3, \frac{7}{2}\}$

31) $x = \{2 + 4\sqrt{2}, 2 - 4\sqrt{2}\}$

32) $a = \{3, -2\}$

33) $x = \{-6, 5\}$

34) $x = \{1 - \sqrt{46}, 1 + \sqrt{46}\}$

35) $a = \{3, 4\}$

36) $x = \{4, 1\}$

37) $a = \{8, -2\}$

38) $n = \{-3, 9\}$

Solve a quadratic equation by factoring

1) $\{-2, 7\}$

2) $\{-3, -5\}$

3) $\{9, -4\}$

4) $\{7, 5\}$

5) $\{-4, -8\}$

6) $\{-\frac{7}{5}, -4\}$

7) $\{-\frac{5}{2}, -\frac{3}{4}\}$

8) $\{-\frac{4}{3}, -2\}$

9) $\{-\frac{1}{2}, -2\}$

10) $\{-\frac{1}{3}, -6\}$

11) $\{2, 0\}$

12) $\{3, -2\}$

13) $\{2, 1\}$

14) $\{-3, -2\}$

15) $\{1, -9\}$

16) $\{2, -12\}$

17) $\{-2, -5\}$

18) $\{-4, -8\}$

19) $\{-4, -7\}$

20) $\{5, -4\}$

21) $\{-5, -3\}$

22) $\{1\}$

23) $\{\frac{6}{5}, \frac{3}{2}\}$

24) $\{\frac{6}{7}, 0\}$

25) $\{-\frac{7}{2}, 2\}$

26) $\{\frac{3}{5}, 2\}$

27) $\{-\frac{4}{3}, -4\}$

28) $\{-8, -7\}$

29) $\{4, -1\}$

30) $\{3, -6\}$

31) $\{3, 8\}$

32) $\{8, 0\}$

Quadratic formula and Transformations of quadratic functions

1) $\{2, -4\}$

2) $\{1, -6\}$

3) $\{\frac{3}{2}, 1\}$

4) $\{3, -\frac{5}{2}\}$

5) $\{2, -\frac{3}{2}\}$

6) $\{6, -2\}$

7) $\{\frac{1+\sqrt{37}}{4}, \frac{1-\sqrt{37}}{4}\}$

8) $\{\frac{-3+i\sqrt{31}}{8}, \frac{-3-i\sqrt{31}}{8}\}$

9) $\{\frac{1+i\sqrt{359}}{20}, \frac{1-i\sqrt{359}}{20}\}$

10) $\{5, 4\}$

11) $\{\frac{1+2\sqrt{3}}{3}, \frac{1-2\sqrt{3}}{3}\}$

12) $\{\frac{1+\sqrt{129}}{8}, \frac{1-\sqrt{129}}{8}\}$

13) $\{\frac{7+\sqrt{17}}{16}, \frac{7-\sqrt{17}}{16}\}$

14) $\{\frac{-1+\sqrt{10}}{2}, \frac{-1-\sqrt{10}}{2}\}$

1)

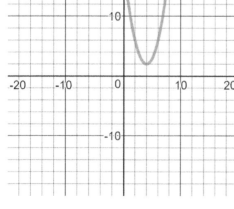

2)

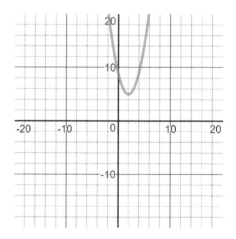

3)

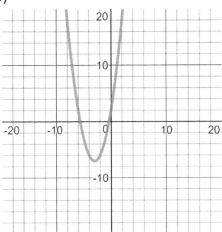

4)

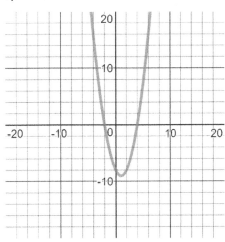

Quadratic formula and the discriminant

1) 1
2) 8
3) −11
4) −15
5) 9
6) 40
7) 17
8) 60
9) −45
10) 57
11) 41
12) 60
13) 96
14) −7

15) 76
16) 189
17) 89
18) 81
19) 13
20) −44
21) 0, *one real solution*
22) 0, *one real solution*
23) −80, *no solution*
24) 0, *one real solution*
25) −224, *no solution*
26) 0, *one real solution*
27) −63, *solution*
28) 0, *one real solution*

Chapter 8:
Polynomial Operations

Topics that you'll learn in this chapter:

- ✓ Simplifying Polynomials
- ✓ Add and Subtract Polynomials
- ✓ Multiply a Polynomial by a Monomial
- ✓ Multiply Two Polynomials
- ✓ Multiply Two Binomials
- ✓ Multiply Polynomials
- ✓ Factor Polynomials
- ✓ Factoring Special Case Polynomials

Simplifying Polynomials

✎ *Simplify each expression.*

1) $5(2x - 10) =$

2) $2x(4x - 2) =$

3) $4x(5x - 3) =$

4) $3x(7x + 3) =$

5) $4x(8x - 4) =$

6) $5x(5x + 4) =$

7) $(2x - 3)(x - 4) =$

8) $(x - 5)(3x + 4) =$

9) $(x - 5)(x - 3) =$

10) $(3x + 8)(3x - 8) =$

11) $(3x - 8)(3x - 4) =$

12) $3x^2 + 3x^2 - 2x^3 =$

13) $2x - x^2 + 6x^3 + 4 =$

14) $5x + 2x^2 - 9x^3 =$

15) $7x^2 + 5x^4 - 2x^3 =$

16) $-3x^2 + 5x^3 + 6x^4 =$

17) $-8x^2 + 2x^3 - 10x^4 + 5x =$

18) $11 - 6x^2 + 5x^2 - 12x^3 + 22 =$

19) $2x^2 - 2x + 3x^3 + 12x - 22x =$

20) $11 - 4x^2 + 3x^2 - 7x^3 + 3 =$

21) $2x^5 - x^3 + 8x^2 - 2x^5 =$

22) $(2x^3 - 1) + (3x^3 - 2x^3) =$

23) $3(4x^4 - 4x^3 - 5x^4) =$

24) $-5(x^6 + 10) - 8(14 - x^6) =$

25) $3x^2 - 5x^3 - x + 10 - 2x^2 =$

26) $11 - 3x^2 + 2x^2 - 5x^3 + 7 =$

27) $(8x^2 - 3x) - (5x - 5 - 8x^2) =$

28) $3x^2 - 5x^3 - x(2x^2 + 4x) =$

29) $4x + 8x^3 - 4 - 3(x^3 - 2) =$

30) $12 + 2x^2 - (8x^3 - x^2 + 6x^3) =$

31) $-2(x^4 + 6) - 5(10 + x^4) =$

32) $(8x^3 - 2x) - (5x - 2x^3) =$

Adding and Subtracting Polynomials

✍ *Add or subtract expressions.*

1) $(-x^2 - 2) + (2x^2 + 1) =$

2) $(2x^2 + 3) - (3 - 4x^2) =$

3) $(2x^3 + 3x^2) - (x^3 + 8) =$

4) $(4x^3 - x^2) + (3x^2 - 5x) =$

5) $(7x^3 + 9x) - (3x^3 + 2) =$

6) $(2x^3 - 2) + (2x^3 + 2) =$

7) $(4x^3 + 5) - (7 - 2x^3) =$

8) $(4x^2 + 2x^3) - (2x^3 + 5) =$

9) $(4x^2 - x) + (3x - 5x^2) =$

10) $(7x + 9) - (3x + 9) =$

11) $(4x^4 - 2x) - (6x - 2x^4) =$

12) $(12x - 4x^3) - (8x^3 + 6x) =$

13) $(2x^3 - 8x^2) - (5x^2 - 3x) =$

14) $(2x^2 - 6) + (9x^2 - 4x^3) =$

15) $(4x^3 + 3x^4) - (x^4 - 5x^3) =$

16) $(-2x^3 - 2x) + (6x - 2x^3) =$

17) $(2x - 4x^4) - (8x^4 + 3x) =$

18) $(2x - 8x^2) - (5x^4 - 3x^2) =$

19) $(2x^3 - 6) + (9x^3 - 4x^2) =$

20) $(4x^3 + 3x^4) - (x^4 - 5x^3) =$

21) $(-2x^2 + 10x^4 + x^3) + (4x^3 + 3x^4 + 8x^2) =$

22) $(3x^2 - 6x^5 - 2x) - (-2x^2 - 6x^5 + 2x) =$

23) $(5x + 9x^3 - 3x^5) + (8x^3 + 3x^5 - 2x) =$

24) $(3x^5 - 2x^4 - 4x) - (4x^2 + 10x^4 - 3x) =$

25) $(13x^2 - 6x^5 - 2x) - (-10x^2 - 11x^5 + 9x) =$

26) $(-12x^4 + 10x^5 + 2x^3) + (14x^3 + 23x^5 + 8x^4) =$

1

1

Multiplying a Polynomial and a Monomial

✎ *Find each product.*

1) $x(x + 3) =$

2) $8(2 - x) =$

3) $2x(2x + 1) =$

4) $x(-x + 3) =$

5) $3x(3x - 2) =$

6) $5(3x - 6y) =$

7) $8x(7x - 4) =$

8) $3x(9x + 2y) =$

9) $6x(x + 2y) =$

10) $9x(2x + 4y) =$

11) $12x(3x + 9) =$

12) $11x(2x - 11y) =$

13) $2x(6x - 6y) =$

14) $2x(3x - 6y + 3) =$

15) $5x(3x^2 + 2y^2) =$

16) $13x(4x + 8y) =$

17) $5(2x^2 - 9y^2) =$

18) $3x(-2x^2y + 3y) =$

19) $-2(2x^2 - 2xy + 2) =$

20) $3(x^2 - 4xy - 8) =$

21) $2x(2x^2 - 3xy + 2x) =$

22) $-x(-x^2 - 5x + 4xy) =$

23) $9(x^2 + xy - 8y^2) =$

24) $3x(2x^2 - 3x + 8) =$

25) $20(2x^2 - 8x - 5) =$

26) $x^2(-x^2 + 3x + 7) =$

27) $x^3(x^2 + 12 - 2x) =$

28) $6x^3(3x^2 - 2x + 2) =$

29) $8x^2(3x^2 - 5xy + 7y^2) =$

30) $2x^2(3x^2 - 5x + 12) =$

31) $2x^3(2x^2 + 5x - 4) =$

32) $5x(6x^2 - 5xy + 2y^2) =$

Multiply Two Polynomials

✏ *Find each product.*

1) $(2x + 2)(6x + 1) =$

2) $(m - 7)(3m + 1) =$

3) $(5x + 2)(7x - 2) =$

4) $(5n - 5)(7n + 6) =$

5) $(3n + 8m)(2n^2 - 4nm + 6m^2) =$

6) $(6x - 6)(-2x^2 - 4x - 8) =$

7) $(-8x^2 - x + 7)(5x + 4) =$

8) $(6x^2 - 8xy + 4y^2)(8x + 8y) =$

9) $(5x^2 + 3y + 5)(y + 9) =$

10) $(x + 5)(y + 3) =$

11) $(6x + 5)(x + 8) =$

12) $(6x^2 + 4y + 6)(y + 4) =$

13) $(y + 6)(y + 4) =$

14) $(7x + 6)(x + 9) =$

15) $(7x^2 + 5y + 7)(y + 5) =$

16) $(x + 8)(x + 6) =$

17) $(8n + 5)(2n + 9) =$

18) $(6x + 7)(x - 7) =$

19) $(y + 9)(y + 7) =$

20) $(9x^2 + 7y + 9)(y + 7) =$

Multiply Two Binomials

✏ *Find each product.*

1) $(x + 2)(x + 2) =$

2) $(x - 3)(x + 2) =$

3) $(x - 2)(x - 4) =$

4) $(x + 3)(x + 2) =$

5) $(x - 4)(x - 5) =$

6) $(x + 5)(x + 2) =$

7) $(x - 6)(x + 3) =$

8) $(x - 8)(x - 4) =$

9) $(x + 2)(x + 8) =$

10) $(x - 2)(x + 4) =$

11) $(x + 4)(x + 4) =$

12) $(x + 5)(x + 5) =$

13) $(x - 3)(x + 3) =$

14) $(x - 2)(x + 2) =$

15) $(x + 3)(x + 3) =$

16) $(x + 4)(x + 6) =$

17) $(x - 7)(x + 7) =$

18) $(x - 7)(x + 2) =$

19) $(2x + 2)(x + 3) =$

20) $(2x - 3)(2x + 4) =$

21) $(x - 8)(2x + 8) =$

22) $(x - 7)(x - 6) =$

23) $(x - 8)(x + 8) =$

24) $(3x - 2)(4x + 2) =$

25) $(2x - 5)(x + 7) =$

26) $(5x - 4)(3x + 3) =$

27) $(6x + 9)(4x + 9) =$

28) $(2x - 6)(5x + 6) =$

29) $(x + 4)(4x - 8) =$

30) $(6x - 4)(6x + 4) =$

31) $(3x + 3)(3x - 4) =$

32) $(x^2 + 2)(x^2 - 2) =$

Operations with Polynomials

✎ *Find each product.*

1) $9(6x + 2) =$ _____

2) $8(3x + 7) =$ _____

3) $5(6x - 1) =$ _____

4) $-3(8x - 3) =$ _____

5) $3x^2(6x - 5) =$ _____

6) $5x^2(7x - 2) =$ _____

7) $6x^3(-3x + 4) =$ _____

8) $-7x^4(2x - 4) =$ _____

9) $8(x^2 + 2x - 3) =$ _____

10) $4(4x^2 - 2x + 1) =$ _____

11) $2(3x^2 + 2x - 2) =$ _____

12) $8x(5x^2 + 3x + 8) =$ _____

13) $(9x + 1)(3x - 1) =$ _____

14) $(4x + 5)(6x - 5) =$ _____

15) $(7x + 3)(5x - 6) =$ _____

16) $(3x - 4)(3x + 8) =$ _____

✎ *Solve each problem.*

17) The measures of two sides of a triangle are $(2x + 3y)$ and $(5x - 2y)$. If the perimeter of the triangle is $(12x + 5y)$, what is the measure of the third side? _____

18) The height of a triangle is $(4x + 5)$ and its base is $(2x - 2)$. What is the area of the triangle? _____

19) One side of a square is $(6x + 9)$. What is the area of the square? _____

20) The length of a rectangle is $(5x - 2y)$ and its width is $(12x + 2y)$. What is the perimeter of the rectangle? _____

21) The side of a cube measures $(x + 2)$. What is the volume of the cube? _____

22) If the perimeter of a rectangle is $(16x + 8y)$ and its width is $(2x + y)$, what is the length of the rectangle? _____

Factor Polynomials

✎ *Factor each trinomial.*

1) $x^2 + 8x + 15 =$

2) $x^2 - 5x + 6 =$

3) $x^2 + 6x + 8 =$

4) $x^2 - 6x + 8 =$

5) $x^2 - 8x + 16 =$

6) $x^2 - 7x + 12 =$

7) $x^2 + 11x + 18 =$

8) $x^2 + 2x - 24 =$

9) $x^2 + 4x - 12 =$

10) $x^2 - 10x + 9 =$

11) $x^2 + 5x - 14 =$

12) $x^2 - 6x - 27 =$

13) $x^2 - 11x - 42 =$

14) $x^2 + 22x + 121 =$

15) $6x^2 + x - 12 =$

16) $x^2 - 17x + 30 =$

17) $3x^2 + 11x - 4 =$

18) $10x^2 + 33x - 7 =$

19) $x^2 + 24x + 144 =$

20) $8x^2 + 10x - 3 =$

✎ *Solve each problem.*

21) The area of a rectangle is $x^2 + 2x - 24$. If the width of rectangle is $x - 4$, what is its length? _____

22) The area of a parallelogram is $8x^2 + 2x - 6$ and its height is $2x + 2$. What is the base of the parallelogram? _____

23) The area of a rectangle is $18x^2 + 9x - 2$. If the width of the rectangle is $6x - 1$, what is its length? _____

Factoring Special Case Polynomials

✎ *Factor each completely.*

1) $4x^2 - 25 =$

2) $x^4 - 100 =$

3) $x^4 - 49 =$

4) $x^2 - 16 =$

5) $3 + 6x + 3x^2 =$

6) $400 - 36x^2 =$

7) $49x^2 - 56x + 16 =$

8) $1 - x^2 =$

9) $81x^4 - 900x^2 =$

10) $10x^2 + 100x + 250 =$

11) $9x^2 - 1 =$

12) $16x^2 - 40x + 25 =$

13) $4x^2 - 25 =$

14) $16x^2 - 9 =$

15) $98x^2 - 200 =$

16) $200x^4 + 80x^3 + 8x^2 =$

17) $343x^2 - 7x^4 =$

18) $16x^2 + 56x + 49 =$

19) $4x^2 - 28x + 49 =$

20) $x^2 - 25y^2 =$

Answers of Worksheets – Chapter 8

Simplifying Polynomials

1) $10x - 50$
2) $8x^2 - 4x$
3) $20x^2 - 12x$
4) $21x^2 + 9x$
5) $32x^2 - 16x$
6) $25x^2 + 20x$
7) $2x^2 - 11x + 12$
8) $3x^2 - 11x - 20$
9) $x^2 - 8x + 15$
10) $9x^2 - 64$
11) $9x^2 - 36x + 32$
12) $-2x^3 + 6x^2$
13) $6x^3 - x^2 + 2x + 4$
14) $-9x^3 + 2x^2 + 5x$
15) $5x^4 - 2x^3 + 7x^2$
16) $6x^4 + 5x^3 - 3x^2$
17) $-10x^4 + 2x^3 - 8x^2 + 5x$
18) $-12x^3 - x^2 + 33$
19) $3x^3 + 2x^2 - 12x$
20) $-7x^3 - x^2 + 14$
21) $-x^3 + 8x^2$
22) $3x^3 - 1$
23) $-3x^4 - 12x^3$
24) $3x^6 - 162$
25) $-5x^3 + x^2 - x + 10$
26) $-5x^3 - x^2 + 18$
27) $16x^2 - 8x + 5$
28) $-5x^3 - x^2$
29) $5x^3 + 4x + 2$
30) $-14x^3 + 3x^2 + 12$
31) $-7x^4 - 62$
32) $10x^3 - 7x$

Adding and Subtracting Polynomials

1) $x^2 - 1$
2) $6x^2$
3) $x^3 + 3x^2 - 8$
4) $4x^3 + 2x^2 - 5x$
5) $4x^3 + 9x - 2$
6) $4x^3$
7) $6x^3 - 2$
8) $4x^2 - 5$
9) $-x^2 + 2x$
10) $4x$
11) $6x^4 - 8x$
12) $-12x^3 + 6x$
13) $2x^3 - 13x^2 + 3x$
14) $-4x^3 + 11x^2 - 6$
15) $2x^4 + 9x^3$
16) $-4x^3 + 4x$
17) $-12x^4 - x$
18) $-5x^4 - 5x^2 + 2x$
19) $11x^3 - 4x^2 - 6$
20) $2x^4 + 9x^3$
21) $13x^4 + 5x^3 + 6x^2$
22) $5x^2 - 4x$
23) $17x^3 + 3x$
24) $3x^5 - 12x^4 - 4x^2 - x$
25) $5x^5 + 23x^2 - 11x$
26) $33x^5 - 4x^4 + 16x^3$

Multiplying a Polynomial and a Monomial

1) $x^2 + 3x$
2) $-8x + 16$
3) $4x^2 + 2x$
4) $-x^2 + 3x$
5) $9x^2 - 6x$
6) $15x - 30y$
7) $56x^2 - 32x$
8) $27x^2 + 6xy$
9) $6x^2 + 12xy$
10) $18x^2 + 36xy$
11) $36x^2 + 108x$
12) $22x^2 - 121xy$
13) $12x^2 - 12xy$
14) $6x^2 - 12xy + 6x$
15) $15x^3 + 10xy^2$
16) $52x^2 + 104xy$
17) $10x^2 - 45y^2$

18) $-6x^3y + 9xy$
19) $-4x^2 + 4xy - 4$
20) $3x^2 - 12xy - 24$
21) $4x^3 - 6x^2y + 4x^2$
22) $x^3 + 5x^2 - 4x^2y$
23) $9x^2 + 9xy - 72y^2$
24) $6x^3 - 9x^2 + 24x$
25) $40x^2 - 160x - 100$
26) $-x^4 + 3x^3 + 7x^2$
27) $x^5 - 2x^4 + 12x^3$
28) $18x^5 - 12x^4 + 12x^3$
29) $24x^4 - 40x^3y + 56x^2y^2$
30) $6x^4 - 10x^3 + 24x^2$
31) $4x^5 + 10x^4 - 8x^3$
32) $30x^3 - 25x^2y + 10xy^2$

Multiply two polynomials

1) $12x^2 + 14x + 2$
2) $3m^2 - 20m - 7$
3) $35x^2 + 4x - 4$
4) $35n^2 - 5n - 30$
5) $54m^3 + 4n^2m - 18nm^2$
6) $-12x^3 - 12x^2 - 24x + 48$
7) $-40x^3 - 37x^2 + 31x + 28$
8) $48x^3 + 32y^3 - 32xy^2$
9) $5x^2y + 45x^2 + 3y^2 + 32y + 45$
10) $xy + 3x + 5y + 15$

11) $6x^2 + 53x + 40$
12) $6x^2y + 4y^2 + 20x^2 + 22y + 24$
13) $y^2 + 10y + 24$
14) $7x^2 + 69x + 54$
15) $7x^2y + 5y^2 + 35x^2 + 32y + 35$
16) $x^2 + 14x + 48$
17) $16n^2 + 82n\ 45$
18) $6x^2 - 35x - 49$
19) $y^2 + 16y + 63$
20) $9x^2y + 7y^2 + 63x^2 + 58y + 63$

Multiply two Binomials

1) $x^2 - x - 6$
2) $x^2 - 6x + 8$
3) $x^2 + 5x + 6$
4) $x^2 - 9x + 20$
5) $x^2 + 7x + 10$
6) $x^2 - 3x - 18$
7) $x^2 - 12x + 32$
8) $x^2 + 10x + 16$
9) $x^2 + 2x - 8$
10) $x^2 + 8x + 6$
11) $x^2 + 10x + 25$
12) $x^2 - 9$
13) $x^2 - 4$
14) $x^2 + 6x + 9$
15) $x^2 + 10x + 24$
16) $x^2 - 49$
17) $x^2 - 5x - 14$
18) $2x^2 + 8x + 6$
19) $4x^2 + 2x - 12$
20) $2x^2 - 8x - 64$
21) $x^2 - 13x + 42$
22) $x^2 - 64$
23) $12x^2 - 2x - 4$
24) $2x^2 + 9x - 35$
25) $15x^2 + 3x - 12$
26) $24x^2 + 90x + 81$
27) $10x^2 - 18x - 36$
28) $4x^2 + 8x - 32$
29) $36x^2 - 16$
30) $9x^2 - 3x - 12$
31) $x^4 - 4$

Operations with Polynomials

1) $54x + 18$
2) $24x + 56$
3) $30x - 5$
4) $-24x + 9$
5) $18x^3 - 15x^2$
6) $35x^3 - 10x^2$
7) $-18x^4 + 24x^3$
8) $-14x^5 + 28x^4$
9) $8x^2 + 16x - 24$
10) $16x^2 - 8x + 4$
11) $6x^2 + 4x - 4$
12) $40x^3 + 24x^2 + 64x$
13) $27x^2 - 6x - 1$
14) $24x^2 + 10x - 25$
15) $35x^2 + 27x - 18$
16) $9x^2 + 12x - 32$
17) $(5x + 4y)$
18) $8x^2 + 2x - 10$
19) $36x^2 + 108x + 81$
20) $34x$
21) $x^3 + 6x^2 + 12x + 6$
22) $(6x + 3y)$

Factor polynomials

1) $(x + 3)(x + 5)$
2) $(x - 2)(x - 3)$
3) $(x + 4)(x + 2)$
4) $(x - 2)(x - 4)$

5) $(x - 4)(x - 4)$

6) $(x - 3)(x - 4)$

7) $(x + 2)(x + 9)$

8) $(x + 6)(x - 4)$

9) $(x - 2)(x + 6)$

10) $(x - 1)(x - 9)$

11) $(x - 2)(x + 7)$

12) $(x - 9)(x + 3)$

13) $(x + 3)(x - 14)$

14) $(x + 11)(x + 11)$

15) $(2x + 3)(3x - 4)$

16) $(x - 15)(x - 2)$

17) $(3x - 1)(x + 4)$

18) $(5x - 1)(2x + 7)$

19) $(x + 12)(x + 12)$

20) $(4x - 1)(2x + 3)$

21) $(x + 6)$

22) $(4x - 3)$

23) $(3x + 2)$

Factoring special case polynomials

1) $(x + 5)(x - 5)$

2) $(x^2 + 10)(x^2 - 10)$

3) $(x^2 + 7)(x^2 - 7)$

4) $(x + 4)(x - 4)$

5) $3(1 + x)^2$

6) $4(10 + 3x)(10 - 3x)$

7) $(7x - 4)^2$

8) $(1 + x)(1 - x)$

9) $9x^2(3x + 10)(3x - 10)$

10) $10(x + 5)^2$

11) $(3x + 1)(3x - 1)$

12) $(4x - 5)^2$

13) $(2x + 5)(2x - 5)$

14) $(4x^2 - 9)$

15) $2(7x + 10)(7x - 10)$

16) $8x^2(5x + 1)^2$

17) $7x^2(7 + x)(7 - x)$

18) $(4x + 7)^2$

19) $(2x - 7)^2$

20) $(-x + 5y)(-x - 5y)$

Chapter 9: Radical Expressions

Topics that you'll learn in this chapter:

- ✓ Simplifying Radical Expressions
- ✓ Simplifying Radical Expressions Involving Fractions
- ✓ Multiplying Radical Expressions
- ✓ Adding and Subtracting Radical Expressions
- ✓ Domain and Range of Radical Functions
- ✓ Solving Radical Equations

Simplifying Radical Expressions

✎ **Simplify.**

1) $\sqrt{35x^2} =$

2) $\sqrt{90x^2} =$

3) $\sqrt[3]{8a} =$

4) $\sqrt{100x^3} =$

5) $\sqrt{125a} =$

6) $\sqrt[3]{88w^3} =$

7) $\sqrt{80x} =$

8) $\sqrt{216v} =$

9) $\sqrt[3]{125x}$

10) $\sqrt{64x^5} =$

11) $\sqrt{4x^2} =$

12) $\sqrt[3]{54a^2}$

13) $\sqrt{405} =$

14) $\sqrt{512p^3} =$

15) $\sqrt{216m^4} =$

16) $\sqrt{264x^3y^3} =$

17) $\sqrt{49x^3y^3} =$

18) $\sqrt{16a^4b^3} =$

19) $\sqrt{20x^3y^3} =$

20) $\sqrt[3]{216yx^3} =$

21) $3\sqrt{75x^2} =$

22) $5\sqrt{80x^2} =$

23) $\sqrt[3]{256x^2y^3} =$

24) $\sqrt[3]{343x^4y^2} =$

25) $4\sqrt{125a} =$

26) $\sqrt[3]{625xy} =$

27) $2\sqrt{8x^2y^3r} =$

28) $4\sqrt{36x^2y^3z^4} =$

29) $2\sqrt[3]{512x^3y^4} =$

30) $5\sqrt{64a^2b^3c^5} =$

31) $2\sqrt[3]{125x^6y^{12}} =$

Multiplying Radical Expressions

🖎 *Simplify.*

1) $\sqrt{5} \times \sqrt{5} =$

2) $\sqrt{5} \times \sqrt{10} =$

3) $\sqrt{2} \times \sqrt{18} =$

4) $\sqrt{14} \times \sqrt{21} =$

5) $\sqrt{5} \times -4\sqrt{20} =$

6) $3\sqrt{12} \times \sqrt{6} =$

7) $5\sqrt{42} \times \sqrt{3} =$

8) $\sqrt{3} \times -\sqrt{25} =$

9) $\sqrt{99} \times \sqrt{48} =$

10) $5\sqrt{45} \times 3\sqrt{176} =$

11) $\sqrt{12}(3 + \sqrt{3}) =$

12) $\sqrt{23x^2} \times \sqrt{23x} =$

13) $-5\sqrt{12} \times -\sqrt{3} =$

14) $2\sqrt{20x^2} \times \sqrt{5x^2} =$

15) $\sqrt{12x^2} \times \sqrt{2x^3} =$

16) $-12\sqrt{7x} \times \sqrt{5x^3} =$

17) $-5\sqrt{9x^3} \times 6\sqrt{3x^2} =$

18) $-2\sqrt{12}(3 + \sqrt{12}) =$

19) $\sqrt{18x}(4 - \sqrt{6x}) =$

20) $\sqrt{3x}(6\sqrt{x^3} + \sqrt{27}) =$

21) $\sqrt{15r}(5 + \sqrt{5}) =$

22) $-5\sqrt{3x} \times 4\sqrt{6x^3} =$

23) $-2\sqrt{18x} \times 4\sqrt{2x}$

24) $-3\sqrt{5v^2}(-3\sqrt{15v}) =$

25) $(\sqrt{5} - \sqrt{3})(\sqrt{5} + \sqrt{3}) =$

26) $(-4\sqrt{6} + 2)(\sqrt{6} - 5) =$

27) $(2 - 2\sqrt{3})(-2 + \sqrt{3}) =$

28) $(11 - 4\sqrt{5})(6 - \sqrt{5}) =$

29) $(-2 - \sqrt{3x})(3 + \sqrt{3x}) =$

30) $(-2 + 3\sqrt{2r})(-2 + \sqrt{2r}) =$

31) $(-4\sqrt{2n} + 2)(-2\sqrt{2} - 4) =$

32) $(-1 + 2\sqrt{3})(2 - 3\sqrt{3x}) =$

Simplifying Radical Expressions Involving Fractions

✍ **Simplify.**

1) $\dfrac{\sqrt{5}}{\sqrt{3}} =$

2) $\dfrac{\sqrt{8}}{\sqrt{100}} =$

3) $\dfrac{\sqrt{2}}{2\sqrt{3}} =$

4) $\dfrac{4}{\sqrt{5}} =$

5) $\dfrac{2\sqrt{5r}}{\sqrt{m^3}} =$

6) $\dfrac{8\sqrt{3}}{\sqrt{k}} =$

7) $\dfrac{6\sqrt{14x^2}}{2\sqrt{18x}} =$

8) $\dfrac{\sqrt{7x^2y^2}}{\sqrt{5x^3y^2}} =$

9) $\dfrac{1}{1+\sqrt{2}} =$

10) $\dfrac{1-5\sqrt{a}}{\sqrt{11a}} =$

11) $\dfrac{\sqrt{a}}{\sqrt{a}+\sqrt{b}} =$

12) $\dfrac{1+\sqrt{2}}{3+\sqrt{5}} =$

13) $\dfrac{2+\sqrt{5}}{6-\sqrt{3}} =$

14) $\dfrac{5}{-3-3\sqrt{3}} =$

15) $\dfrac{2}{3+\sqrt{5}} =$

16) $\dfrac{\sqrt{7}-\sqrt{3}}{\sqrt{3}-\sqrt{7}} =$

17) $\dfrac{\sqrt{7}+\sqrt{5}}{\sqrt{5}+\sqrt{2}} =$

18) $\dfrac{3\sqrt{2}-\sqrt{7}}{4\sqrt{2}+\sqrt{5}} =$

19) $\dfrac{\sqrt{5}+2\sqrt{2}}{4-\sqrt{5}} =$

20) $\dfrac{5\sqrt{3}-3\sqrt{2}}{3\sqrt{2}-2\sqrt{3}} =$

21) $\dfrac{\sqrt{8a^5b^3}}{\sqrt{2ab^2}} =$

22) $\dfrac{6\sqrt{45x^3}}{3\sqrt{5x}} =$

Adding and Subtracting Radical Expressions

✎ *Simplify.*

1) $\sqrt{3} + \sqrt{27} =$

2) $3\sqrt{8} + 3\sqrt{2} =$

3) $4\sqrt{3} - 2\sqrt{12} =$

4) $3\sqrt{18} - 2\sqrt{2} =$

5) $2\sqrt{45} - 2\sqrt{5} =$

6) $-\sqrt{12} - 5\sqrt{3} =$

7) $-4\sqrt{2} - 5\sqrt{32} =$

8) $5\sqrt{10} + 2\sqrt{40} =$

9) $4\sqrt{12} - 3\sqrt{27} =$

10) $-3\sqrt{2} + 4\sqrt{18} =$

11) $-10\sqrt{7} + 6\sqrt{28} =$

12) $5\sqrt{3} - \sqrt{27} =$

13) $-\sqrt{12} + 3\sqrt{3} =$

14) $-3\sqrt{6} - \sqrt{54} =$

15) $3\sqrt{8} + 3\sqrt{2} =$

16) $2\sqrt{12} - 3\sqrt{27} =$

17) $\sqrt{50} - \sqrt{32} =$

18) $4\sqrt{8} - 6\sqrt{2} =$

19) $-4\sqrt{12} + 12\sqrt{108} =$

20) $2\sqrt{45} - 2\sqrt{5} =$

21) $7\sqrt{18} - 3\sqrt{2} =$

22) $-12\sqrt{35} + 7\sqrt{140} =$

23) $-6\sqrt{19} - 3\sqrt{76} =$

24) $-\sqrt{54x} - 3\sqrt{6x} =$

25) $\sqrt{5y^2} + y\sqrt{45} =$

26) $\sqrt{8mn^2} + 2n\sqrt{18m} =$

27) $-8\sqrt{27a} - 5\sqrt{3a} =$

28) $-4\sqrt{7ab} - \sqrt{28ab} =$

29) $\sqrt{27a^2b} + a\sqrt{12b} =$

30) $3\sqrt{6a^3} - 2\sqrt{24a^3} + 2a\sqrt{54a} =$

Domain and Range of Radical Functions

✎ *Identify the domain and range of each function.*

1) $y = \sqrt{x + 2} - 3$

2) $y = \sqrt[3]{x - 1} - 1$

3) $y = \sqrt{x - 2} + 5$

4) $y = \sqrt[3]{(x + 1)} - 4$

5) $y = 3\sqrt{3x + 6} + 5$

6) $y = \sqrt[3]{(2x - 1)} - 4$

7) $y = 6\sqrt{3x^2 + 6} + 5$

8) $y = \sqrt[3]{(2x^2 - 2)} - 4$

9) $y = 4\sqrt{4x^3 + 32} - 1$

10) $y = \sqrt[3]{(4x + 8)} - 2x$

11) $y = 7\sqrt{-2(2x + 4)} + 1$

12) $y = \sqrt[5]{(4x^2 - 5)} - 2$

13) $y = 2x\sqrt{5x^4 + 6} - 2x$

14) $y = 6\sqrt[3]{(8x^6 + 2x + 8)} - 2$

✎ *Sketch the graph of each function.*

5) $y = \sqrt{x} + 8$

6) $y = 2\sqrt{x} - 4$

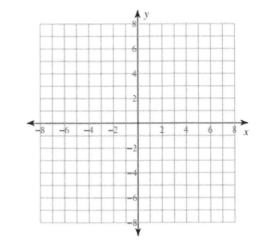

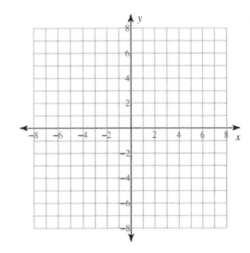

Solving Radical Equations

✎ **Solve each equation. Remember to check for extraneous solutions.**

1) $\sqrt{a} = 5$

2) $\sqrt{v} = 3$

3) $\sqrt{r} = 4$

4) $2 = 4\sqrt{x}$

5) $\sqrt{x + 1} = 9$

6) $1 = \sqrt{x - 5}$

7) $6 = \sqrt{r - 2}$

8) $\sqrt{x - 6} = 8$

9) $5 = \sqrt{x - 3}$

10) $\sqrt{m + 8} = 8$

11) $10\sqrt{9a} = 60$

12) $5\sqrt{3x} = 15$

13) $1 = \sqrt{3x - 5}$

14) $\sqrt{12 - x} = x$

15) $\sqrt{r + 3} - 1 = 7$

16) $-12 = -6\sqrt{r + 4}$

17) $20 = 2\sqrt{36v}$

18) $x = \sqrt{42 - x}$

19) $\sqrt{110 - a} = a$

20) $\sqrt{2n - 12} = 2$

21) $\sqrt{3r - 5} = r - 3$

22) $\sqrt{-16 + 10x} = x$

23) $\sqrt{3x + 12} = \sqrt{x + 8}$

24) $\sqrt{v} = \sqrt{2v - 6}$

25) $\sqrt{11 - x} = \sqrt{x - 7}$

26) $\sqrt{m + 8} = \sqrt{3m + 8}$

27) $\sqrt{2r + 40} = \sqrt{-16 - 2r}$

28) $\sqrt{k + 3} = \sqrt{1 - k}$

29) $-10\sqrt{x - 10} = -60$

30) $\sqrt{72 - x} = \sqrt{\dfrac{x}{5}}$

Answers of Worksheets – Chapter 9

Simplifying radical expressions

1) $x\sqrt{35}$

2) $3x\sqrt{10}$

3) $2\sqrt[3]{a}$

4) $10x\sqrt{x}$

5) $5\sqrt{5a}$

6) $2w\sqrt[3]{11}$

7) $4\sqrt{5x}$

8) $6\sqrt{6v}$

9) $5\sqrt[3]{x}$

10) $8x^2\sqrt{x}$

11) $2x$

12) $3\sqrt[3]{2a^2}$

13) $9\sqrt{5}$

14) $16p\sqrt{2p}$

15) $6m^2\sqrt{6}$

16) $2x.y\sqrt{66xy}$

17) $7xy\sqrt{xy}$

18) $4a^2b\sqrt{b}$

19) $2xy\sqrt{5xy}$

20) $6x\sqrt[3]{y}$

21) $15x\sqrt{3}$

22) $20x\sqrt{5}$

23) $16y\sqrt[3]{x^2}$

24) $7x\sqrt[3]{xy^2}$

25) $20\sqrt{5a}$

26) $5\sqrt[3]{5xy}$

27) $4xy\sqrt{2yr}$

28) $24\,x\,yz^2\sqrt{y}$

29) $16xy\sqrt[3]{y}$

30) $40abc^2\sqrt{bc}$

31) $10x^2y^4$

Multiplying radical expressions

1) 5

2) $5\sqrt{2}$

3) 6

4) $7\sqrt{6}$

5) -40

6) $18\sqrt{2}$

7) $15\sqrt{14}$

8) $-5\sqrt{3}$

9) $12\sqrt{33}$

10) $180\sqrt{55}$

11) $6\sqrt{3}+6$

12) $23x\sqrt{x}$

13) 30

14) $20x^2$

15) $2x\sqrt{6x}$

16) $-12x^2\sqrt{35}$

17) $-90x^2\sqrt{3x}$

18) $-12\sqrt{3}-24$

19) $6\sqrt{2x}-6x\sqrt{3}$

20) $54x^2$

21) $5\sqrt{15r}+3\sqrt{5r}$

22) $-60x^2\sqrt{2}$

23) $-48x$

24) $45v\sqrt{3v}$

25) 2

26) $22\sqrt{3} - 34$

27) $6\sqrt{3} - 10$

28) $86 - 35\sqrt{5}$

29) $-3x - 5\sqrt{3x} - 6$

30) $12r - 8\sqrt{2r} + 4$

31) $16\sqrt{n} + 16\sqrt{2n} - 4\sqrt{2} - 8$

32) $-2 + 3\sqrt{3x} + 4\sqrt{3} - 18\sqrt{x}$

Simplifying radical expressions involving fractions

1) $\dfrac{\sqrt{15}}{3}$

2) $\dfrac{\sqrt{2}}{5}$

3) $\dfrac{\sqrt{6}}{6}$

4) $\dfrac{4\sqrt{5}}{5}$

5) $\dfrac{2\sqrt{5mr}}{m^2}$

6) $\dfrac{8\sqrt{3k}}{k}$

7) $\sqrt{7x}$

8) $\dfrac{\sqrt{35x}}{5x}$

9) $-1 + \sqrt{2}$

10) $\dfrac{\sqrt{11a} - 5a\sqrt{11}}{11a}$

11) $\dfrac{a - \sqrt{ab}}{a - b}$

12) $\dfrac{3 - \sqrt{5} + 3\sqrt{2} - \sqrt{10}}{4}$

13) $\dfrac{12 + 2\sqrt{3} + 6\sqrt{5} + \sqrt{15}}{33}$

14) $\dfrac{5 - 5\sqrt{5}}{6}$

15) $-3 + \sqrt{5}$

16) -1

17) $\dfrac{\sqrt{35} - \sqrt{14} + 5 - \sqrt{10}}{3}$

18) $\dfrac{24 - 3\sqrt{10} - 4\sqrt{14} + \sqrt{35}}{27}$

19) $\dfrac{4\sqrt{5} + 5 + 8\sqrt{2} + 2\sqrt{10}}{11}$

20) $\dfrac{3\sqrt{6} + 4}{2}$

21) $2a^2\sqrt{b}$

22) $6x$

Adding and subtracting radical expressions

1) $4\sqrt{3}$

2) $9\sqrt{2}$

3) 0

4) $7\sqrt{2}$

5) $4\sqrt{5}$

6) $-7\sqrt{3}$

7) $-24\sqrt{2}$

8) $9\sqrt{10}$

9) $-\sqrt{3}$

10) $9\sqrt{2}$

11) $2\sqrt{7}$

12) $2\sqrt{3}$

13) $\sqrt{3}$

14) 0

15) $9\sqrt{2}$

16) $-5\sqrt{3}$

17) $\sqrt{2}$

18) $2\sqrt{2}$

19) $64\sqrt{3}$

20) $4\sqrt{5}$

21) $18\sqrt{2}$

22) $2\sqrt{35}$

23) $-12\sqrt{19}$

24) $-6\sqrt{6x}$

25) $4y\sqrt{5}$

26) $8n\sqrt{2m}$

27) $-29\sqrt{3a}$

28) $-8\sqrt{7ab}$

29) $5a\sqrt{3b}$

30) $5a\sqrt{6a}$

Domain and range of radical functions

1) domain: $x \geq -2$
   range: $y \geq -3$

2) domain: {all real numbers}
   range: {all real numbers}

3) domain: $x \geq 2$
   range: $y \geq 5$

4) domain: {all real numbers}
   range: {all real numbers}

5) domain: $x \geq -2$
   range: $y \geq 5$

6) domain: {all real numbers}
   range: {all real numbers}

7) domain: {all real numbers}
   range: {all real numbers}

8) domain: {all real numbers}
   range: {all real numbers}

9) domain: $x \geq -2$
   range: $y \geq -1$

10) domain: {all real numbers}
    range: {all real numbers}

11) domain: $x \leq -2$
    range: $y \geq 1$

12) domain: {all real numbers}
    range: {all real numbers}

13) domain: {all real numbers}
    range: {all real numbers}

14) domain: {all real numbers}
    range: {all real numbers}

5)

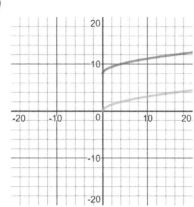

6)

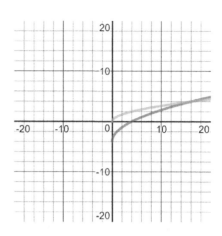

Solving radical equations

1) {25}
2) {9}
3) {16}
4) {$\frac{1}{4}$}
5) {80}
6) {6}
7) {38}
8) {70}
9) {28}
10) {56}

11) {4}
12) {3}
13) {2}
14) {3}
15) {61}
16) {0}
17) {$\frac{25}{9}$}
18) {6}
19) {10}
20) {8}

21) {4}
22) {2, 8}
23) {−2}
24) {6}
25) {9}
26) {0}
27) {−14}
28) {−1}
29) {46}
30) {60}

Chapter 10: Rational Expressions

Topics that you'll learn in this chapter:

- ✓ Simplifying and Graphing Rational Expressions
- ✓ Adding and Subtracting Rational Expressions
- ✓ Multiplying and Dividing Rational Expressions
- ✓ Solving Rational Equations and Complex Fractions

Simplifying and Graphing Rational Expressions

✎ *Simplify.*

1) $\dfrac{x+3}{3x+9} =$

2) $\dfrac{2x^2 - 2x - 12}{x - 3} =$

3) $\dfrac{16}{4x - 4} =$

4) $\dfrac{36x^3}{42x^3} =$

5) $\dfrac{x^2 - 3x - 4}{x^2 + 2x - 24} =$

6) $\dfrac{81x^3}{18x} =$

7) $\dfrac{x - 3}{x^2 - x - 6} =$

8) $\dfrac{x^2 - 3x - 28}{x - 7} =$

9) $\dfrac{6x + 18}{30} =$

10) $\dfrac{16}{4x - 4} =$

✎ *Identify the points of discontinuity, holes, vertical asymptotes, x–intercepts, and horizontal asymptote of each.*

11) $f(x) = \dfrac{x^3 - x^2 - 6x}{-3x^3 - 3x + 18} =$

12) $f(x) = \dfrac{x^2 + x - 6}{-4x^2 - 16x - 12} =$

13) $f(x) = \dfrac{x - 2}{x - 4} =$

14) $f(x) = \dfrac{1}{3x^2 + 3x - 18} =$

✎ *Graph rational expressions.*

15) $f(x) = \dfrac{x^2 + 2x - 4}{x - 2}$

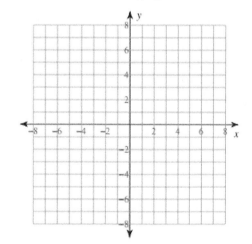

16) $f(x) = \dfrac{4x^3 - 16x + 64}{x^2 - 2x - 4}$

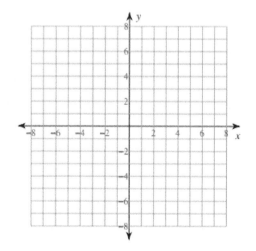

Adding and Subtracting Rational Expressions

✎ *Simplify each expression.*

1) $\dfrac{2}{6x+10} + \dfrac{x-6}{6x+10} =$

2) $\dfrac{x+2}{x-4} + \dfrac{x-2}{x+3} =$

3) $\dfrac{3}{x+7} - \dfrac{4}{x-8} =$

4) $\dfrac{x-7}{x^2-16} - \dfrac{x-1}{16-x^2} =$

5) $\dfrac{5}{x+5} + \dfrac{4x}{2x+6} =$

6) $2 + \dfrac{x-3}{x+1} =$

7) $\dfrac{2x}{5x+4} + \dfrac{6x}{2x+3} =$

8) $\dfrac{5xy}{x^2-y^2} - \dfrac{x-y}{x+y} =$

9) $\dfrac{2}{x^2-5x+4} + \dfrac{-2}{x^2-4} =$

10) $\dfrac{4}{x+1} - \dfrac{2}{x+2} =$

11) $\dfrac{5x+5}{5x^2+35x-40} + \dfrac{7x}{3x} =$

12) $3 + \dfrac{x}{x+2} - \dfrac{2}{x^2-4} =$

13) $\dfrac{4}{x+1} - \dfrac{2}{x+2} =$

14) $\dfrac{2}{3x^2+12x} + \dfrac{8}{2x} =$

15) $\dfrac{2x}{5x+4} + \dfrac{6x}{2x+3} =$

16) $\dfrac{x+5}{4x^2+20x} - \dfrac{x-5}{4x^2+20x} =$

Multiplying and Dividing Rational Expressions

✎ *Simplify each expression.*

1) $\dfrac{12x}{14} \times \dfrac{14}{16x} =$

2) $\dfrac{79x}{25} \times \dfrac{85}{27x^2} =$

3) $\dfrac{96}{38x} \times \dfrac{25}{45} =$

4) $\dfrac{84}{3} \times \dfrac{48x}{95} =$

5) $\dfrac{53}{43} \times \dfrac{46x^2}{31} =$

6) $\dfrac{93}{21x} \times \dfrac{34x}{51x} =$

7) $\dfrac{5x + 50}{x + 10} \times \dfrac{x - 2}{5} =$

8) $\dfrac{x - 7}{x + 6} \times \dfrac{10x + 60}{x - 7} =$

9) $\dfrac{1}{x + 10} \times \dfrac{10x + 30}{x + 3} =$

10) $\dfrac{8\,(x+1)}{7x} \times \dfrac{9}{8\,(x+1)} =$

11) $\dfrac{2\,(x + 6)}{4} \times \dfrac{x - 3}{2\,(x - 1)} =$

12) $\dfrac{9\,(x + 4)}{x + 4} \times \dfrac{9x}{9\,(x - 5)} =$

13) $\dfrac{3x^2 + 18x}{x + 6} \times \dfrac{1}{x + 8} =$

14) $\dfrac{21x^2 - 21x}{18x^2 - 18x} \times \dfrac{6x}{6x^2} =$

15) $\dfrac{1}{x - 9} \times \dfrac{x^2 + 6x - 27}{x + 9} =$

16) $\dfrac{x^2 - 10x + 25}{10x - 100} \times \dfrac{x - 10}{45 - 9x} =$

✎ *Divide.*

1) $\dfrac{8 + 2x - x^2}{x^2 - 2x - 8} \div \dfrac{4x}{x + 6} =$

2) $\dfrac{12x}{3} \div \dfrac{5}{8} =$

3) $\dfrac{9a}{a + 5} \div \dfrac{9a}{2a + 10} =$

4) $\dfrac{10x^2}{7} \div \dfrac{3n}{12} =$

5) $\dfrac{11x}{x - 7} \div \dfrac{11x}{12x - 84} =$

6) $\dfrac{x + 10}{9x^2 - 90x} \div \dfrac{1}{9x} =$

7) $\dfrac{x - 2}{x + 6x - 16} \div \dfrac{11x}{x + 9} =$

8) $\dfrac{3x}{x - 5} \div \dfrac{3x}{10x - 50} =$

9) $\dfrac{x + 5}{x + 13x + 40} \div \dfrac{4x}{x + 9} =$

10) $\dfrac{x + 4}{x + 14x + 40} \div \dfrac{6x}{x + 9} =$

11) $\dfrac{14x + 12}{3} \div \dfrac{63x + 54}{3x} =$

12) $\dfrac{7x^3 + 49x^2}{x^2 + 12x + 35} \div \dfrac{2}{2x^3 - 12x^2} =$

13) $\dfrac{x^2 + 10x + 16}{x^2 + 6x + 8} \div \dfrac{1}{x + 8} =$

14) $\dfrac{x^2 - 2x - 15}{8x + 20} \div \dfrac{2}{4x + 10} =$

15) $\dfrac{x - 4}{x^2 - 2x - 8} \div \dfrac{1}{x - 5} =$

16) $\dfrac{1}{2x} \div \dfrac{8x}{2x^2 + 16x} =$

Solving Rational Equations and Complex Fractions

✎ **Solve each equation. Remember to check for extraneous solutions.**

1) $\dfrac{2x-3}{x+1} = \dfrac{x+6}{x-2}$

2) $\dfrac{1}{x} = \dfrac{6}{5x} + 1$

3) $\dfrac{2x-3}{x+1} = \dfrac{x+6}{x-2}$

4) $\dfrac{1}{6b^2} + \dfrac{1}{6b} = \dfrac{1}{b^2}$

5) $\dfrac{3x-2}{9x+1} = \dfrac{2x-5}{6x-5}$

6) $\dfrac{1}{n^2} + \dfrac{1}{n} = \dfrac{1}{2n^2}$

7) $\dfrac{1}{8b^2} = \dfrac{1}{4b^2} - \dfrac{1}{b}$

8) $\dfrac{1}{n-8} - 1 = \dfrac{7}{n-8}$

9) $\dfrac{5}{r-2} = -\dfrac{10}{r+2} + 7$

10) $1 = \dfrac{1}{x^2+2x} + \dfrac{x-1}{x}$

11) $\dfrac{1}{x} = 8 + \dfrac{6}{9x}$

12) $\dfrac{x+5}{x^2-2x} - 1 = \dfrac{1}{x^2-2x}$

13) $\dfrac{x-2}{x+3} - 1 = \dfrac{1}{x+2}$

14) $\dfrac{1}{6x^2} = \dfrac{1}{3x^2} - \dfrac{1}{x}$

15) $\dfrac{x+5}{x^2-x} = \dfrac{1}{x^2+x} - \dfrac{x-6}{x+1}$

16) $1 = \dfrac{1}{x^2-2x} + \dfrac{x-1}{x}$

✎ **Simplify each expression.**

17) $\dfrac{-1\frac{11}{12}}{-3} =$

18) $\dfrac{\frac{4}{5}}{\frac{2}{25} - \frac{5}{16}} =$

19) $\dfrac{\frac{14}{3}}{-6\frac{2}{11}} =$

20) $\dfrac{9}{\frac{9}{x} + \frac{2}{3x}} =$

21) $\dfrac{x^2}{\frac{4}{5} - \frac{4}{x}} =$

22) $\dfrac{\frac{4}{x-3} - \frac{2}{x+2}}{\frac{8}{x^2+6x+8}} =$

23) $\dfrac{\frac{16}{x-1}}{\frac{16}{5} - \frac{16}{25}} =$

24) $\dfrac{2 + \frac{6}{x-4}}{2 - \frac{4}{x-4}} =$

25) $\dfrac{\frac{1}{2} - \frac{x+5}{4}}{\frac{x^2}{2} - \frac{5}{2}} =$

26) $\dfrac{\frac{x-6}{2} - \frac{x-2}{x-6}}{\frac{36}{x-2} + \frac{4}{9}} =$

Answers of Worksheets – Chapter 10

Simplifying and Graphing rational expressions

1) $\frac{1}{3}$

2) $2(x-3)(x+2)$

3) $\frac{4}{x-1}$

4) $\frac{6}{7}$

5) $\frac{x+1}{x+6}$

6) $\frac{9x^2}{2}$

7) $\frac{x+3}{5}$

8) $x+4$

9) $\frac{x+3}{8}$

10) $\frac{4}{x-1}$

11) Discontinuities: $-3, 2$

Vertical Asym: $x=-3, x=2$

Holes: None

Horz. Asym: None

X–intercepts: $0, -2, 3$

12) Discontinuitiesâ $-1, -3$

Vertical Asymâ $x=-1$

Holes $x=-3$

Horz. Asym: $y=-\frac{1}{4}$

X–interceptsâ 2

13) Discontinuities: 4

Vertical Asym: $x=4$

Holes: None

Horz. Asym: $y=1$

X–intercepts: 2

14) Discontinuities: $-3, 2$

Vertical Asym: $x=-3, x=2$

Holes: None

Horz. Asym: $y=0$

X–intercepts: None

15)

16)

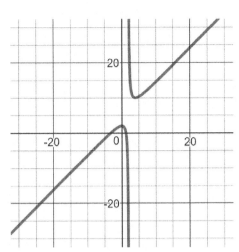
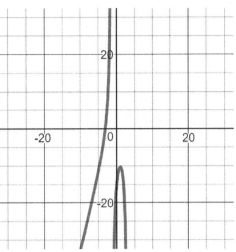

Adding and subtracting rational expressions

1) $\dfrac{-4+x}{6x+10}$

2) $\dfrac{2x^2 - x + 14}{(x-4)(x+3)}$

3) $\dfrac{7x+4}{(x+7)(x-8)}$

4) $\dfrac{2}{x+4}$

5) $\dfrac{x-5}{x+2}$

6) $\dfrac{3x-1}{x+1}$

7) $\dfrac{34x^2 + 30x}{(5x+4)(2x+3)}$

8) $\dfrac{-x^2 + 7xy - y^2}{(x-y)(x+y)}$

9) $\dfrac{10x-16}{(x^2-5x+4)(x^2-4)}$

10) $\dfrac{2x+6}{(x+1)(x+2)}$

11) $\dfrac{52x - 53 + 7x^2}{3(x+8)(x-1)}$

12) $\dfrac{4x^2 - 2x - 14}{(x+2)(x-2)}$

13) $\dfrac{2x+6}{(x+1)(x+2)}$

14) $\dfrac{50+12x}{3x(x+4)}$

15) $\dfrac{34x^2 + 30x}{(5x+4)(2x+3)}$

16) $\dfrac{5}{2x^2+10x}$

Multiplying and Dividing rational expressions

1) $\dfrac{4720}{3267}$

2) $\dfrac{1343}{135x}$

3) $\dfrac{80}{57x}$

4) $\dfrac{1344x}{95}$

5) $\dfrac{2438x^2}{1333}$

6) $\dfrac{62}{21x}$

7) $X-2$

8) 10

9) $\dfrac{10}{x+10}$

10) $\dfrac{9}{7x}$

11) $\dfrac{x+6}{4}$

12) $\dfrac{9x}{x-5}$

13) $\dfrac{3x}{x+8}$

14) $\dfrac{7}{6x}$

15) $\dfrac{x-3}{x-9}$

16) $-\dfrac{(x-5)}{90}$

17) $\dfrac{32x}{5}$

18) $6x^2$

19) 2

20) $\frac{40n}{7}$

21) 12

22) $\frac{x+10}{x-10}$

23) $\frac{x+9}{11x\,(x+8)}$

24) 10

25) $\frac{2x}{9}$

26) $\frac{x+9}{6x\,(x+10)}$

27) $\frac{2x}{9}$

28) $\frac{14x^4}{x+5}$

29) x + 8

30) $\frac{(x+3)(x-5)}{4}$

31) $\frac{x-5}{x+2}$

32) $\frac{x+8}{8x}$

Solving rational equations and complex fractions

1) $\{\frac{1}{2}\}$

2) $\{-\frac{1}{5}\}$

3) $\{0, 14\}$

4) $\{-\frac{15}{16}\}$

5) $\{\frac{1}{6}\}$

6) $\{-\frac{1}{2}\}$

7) $\{\frac{1}{8}\}$

8) $\{2\}$

9) $\{-\frac{6}{7}, 3\}$

10) $\{-1\}$

11) $\{\frac{1}{24}\}$

12) $\{4, -1\}$

13) $\{-\frac{19}{8}\}$

14) $\{\frac{1}{6}\}$

15) $\{-\frac{1}{4}\}$

16) $\{4, 1\}$

17) $\frac{23}{36}$

18) $-\frac{320}{93}$

19) $-\frac{77}{102}$

20) $\frac{27x}{29}$

21) $\frac{5x^2}{4x-20}$

22) $\frac{(x+7)(x+4)}{4\,(x-3)}$

23) $\frac{25}{4x-4}$

24) $\frac{x-1}{x-6}$

25) $\frac{-3-x}{2x^2-10}$

26) $\frac{3x^3-60x^2+252x-288-x}{584x+8x^2-3792}$

Chapter 11: Statistics and Probabilities

Topics that you'll learn in this chapter:

- ✓ Probability Problems
- ✓ Permutations
- ✓ Combination

Probability Problems

✎ *Solve.*

1) A number is chosen at random from 1 to 10. Find the probability of selecting number 4 or smaller numbers. _____

2) Bag A contains 9 red marbles and 3 green marbles. Bag B contains 9 black marbles and 6 orange marbles. What is the probability of selecting a green marble at random from bag A? What is the probability of selecting a black marble at random from Bag B? _____ _____

3) A number is chosen at random from 1 to 50. What is the probability of selecting multiples of 10. _____

4) A card is chosen from a well-shuffled deck of 52 cards. What is the probability that the card will be a king OR a queen? _____

5) A number is chosen at random from 1 to 10. What is the probability of selecting a multiple of 3. _____

A spinner, numbered 1-8, is spun once. What is the probability of spinning ...

6) an EVEN number? _____   7) a multiple of 3? _____

8) a PRIME number? _____   9) number 9? _____

Factorials

✎ *Determine the value for each expression.*

1) $3! + 2! =$

2) $3! + 6! =$

3) $(3!)^2 =$

4) $5! + 4! =$

5) $4! - 5! + 4 =$

6) $2! \times 5 - 12 =$

7) $(2! + 1!)^3 =$

8) $(3! + 0!)^3 =$

9) $(2!\, 0!)^4 - 1 =$

10) $\dfrac{7!}{4!} =$

11) $\dfrac{9!}{6!} =$

12) $\dfrac{8!}{5!} =$

13) $\dfrac{7!}{5!} =$

14) $\dfrac{20!}{18!} =$

15) $\dfrac{10!}{8!} =$

16) $\dfrac{(5+1!)^3}{3!} =$

17) $\dfrac{25!}{20!} =$

18) $\dfrac{22!}{18!5!} =$

19) $\dfrac{10!}{8!2!} =$

20) $\dfrac{100!}{97!} =$

21) $\dfrac{14!}{10!4!} =$

22) $\dfrac{14!}{9!3!} =$

23) $\dfrac{55!}{53!} =$

24) $\dfrac{(2 \cdot 3)!}{3!} =$

25) $\dfrac{4!(9n-1)!}{(9n)!} =$

26) $\dfrac{n(3n+8)!}{(3n+9)!} =$

27) $\dfrac{(n-2)!(n-1)}{(n+1)!} =$

Combinations and Permutations

✍ *Calculate the value of each.*

1) $4! = $ _____

2) $4! \times 3! = $ _____

3) $5! = $ _____

4) $6! + 3! = $ _____

5) $7! = $ _____

6) $8! = $ _____

7) $4! + 4! = $ _____

8) $4! - 3! = $ _____

✍ *Solve each word problems.*

9) Susan is baking cookies. She uses sugar, flour, butter, and eggs. How many different orders of ingredients can she try? _____

10) Jason is planning for his vacation. He wants to go to museum, watch a movie, go to the beach, and play volleyball. How many different ways of ordering are there for him? _____

11) How many 5-digit numbers can be named using the digits 1, 2, 3, 4, and 5 without repetition? _____

12) In how many ways can 5 boys be arranged in a straight line? _____

13) In how many ways can 4 athletes be arranged in a straight line? _____

14) A professor is going to arrange her 7 students in a straight line. In how many ways can she do this? _____

15) How many code symbols can be formed with the letters for the word WHITE? _____

16) In how many ways a team of 8 basketball players can to choose a captain and co-captain? _____

Answers of Worksheets – Chapter 11

Probability Problems

1) $\frac{2}{5}$

2) $\frac{1}{4}, \frac{3}{5}$

3) $\frac{1}{5}$

4) $\frac{2}{13}$

5) $\frac{3}{10}$

6) $\frac{1}{2}$

7) $\frac{1}{4}$

8) $\frac{1}{2}$

9) 0

Factorials

1) 8
2) 726
3) 36
4) 144
5) −92
6) −2
7) 27
8) 125
9) 15
10) 210

11) 504
12) 336
13) 42
14) 380
15) 90
16) 36
17) 6,375,600
18) 1,463
19) 45
20) 970,200

21) 1,001
22) 40,040
23) 2,970
24) 120
25) $\frac{8}{3n}$
26) $\frac{n}{3(n+3)}$
27) $\frac{1}{n(n+1)}$

Combinations and Permutations

1) 24
2) 144
3) 120
4) 726
5) 5,040
6) 40,320
7) 48
8) 18
9) 24
10) 24
11) 120
12) 120
13) 24
14) 5,040
15) 120
16) 56

"Effortless Math" Publications

Effortless Math authors' team strives to prepare and publish the best quality Mathematics learning resources to make learning Math easier for all. We hope that our publications help you or your student learn Math in an effective way.

We all in Effortless Math wish you good luck and successful studies!

Effortless Math Authors

www.EffortlessMath.com

... So Much More Online!

✓ FREE Math lessons

✓ More Math learning books!

✓ Mathematics Worksheets

✓ Online Math Tutors

Need a PDF version of this book?

Please visit www.EffortlessMath.com

Made in the USA
Las Vegas, NV
03 March 2021